朗文

英漢圖片詞典

LONGMAN ENGLISH-CHINESE
PHOTO DICTIONARY

Marilyn S. Rosenthal and Daniel B. Freeman

Translated by
Leong Hoi Chong

D1370058

Longman 朗文

© Longman Inc. 1989
© Longman Group (Far East) Ltd 1989

Published by
Longman Group (Far East) Ltd
18/F., Cornwall House
Tong Chong Street
Quarry Bay
Hong Kong
Tel: 5-8118168
Fax: 5-657440 G2&3
Telex: 73051 LGHK HX

朗文出版（遠東）有限公司
香港鰂魚涌糖廠街
康和大廈十八樓
電話：5-8118168
圖文傳眞：5-657440 G2&3
電傳：73051 LGHK HX

First published 1989
Reprinted 1989
一九八九年初版
一九八九年重印

ISBN 962 359 038 5 （香港版）
ISBN 962 359 117 9 （台灣版）
ISBN 962 359 118 7 （簡體字版）

Produced by Longman Group (Far East) Ltd.
Printed in Hong Kong by Sheck Wah Tong Printing Press Ltd.
承印：香港石華堂印刷有限公司

FOREWORD　前　言

朗文英漢圖片詞典，不同於一般的圖畫詞典。不同點有五：

1. 特爲不同程度的中小學生、有志於自修英文的成年人及移民而編。

2. 根據詞典每一單元的圖片內容，附加英文會話練習，在看圖識字的基礎上，進而看圖造句，看圖練對話。

3. 可憑圖畫和所給詞彙，進行拼字、默寫、聆聽、造句、講故事、練對話等等，接受聽、說、讀、寫四方面的基礎訓練。

4. 提供大量的美、加生活詞彙、地區和城市名稱。方便移民自修英文，可學到諸如上銀行、郵局辦事，去醫院看病，到超級市場購物以及火車站、飛機場、家庭用品各方面的用語。

5. 提供錄音帶，領讀英文詞彙和句型，可學習英語的正確發音。

本詞典共收 2,000 多個單詞和詞組，分 68 個單元，800 餘幅彩色圖片、100 多種不同英文句型和 500 多句對話練習。

如果你從這本詞典學到像 broccoli（西蘭花）、asparagus（蘆筍）、pot holder（廚房用隔熱手套）、casserole（燉鍋）、three-pronged plug（三腳插頭）這一類的詞；或者，如果你開着汽車，想找個停車場，能問路人說："Is there a parking lot near here?" 你一定同意：這不是一本普通的圖畫詞典。

朗文出版（遠東）有限公司
辭書/翻譯出版部
一九八九年五月

CONTENTS 目 錄

NUMBERS 數字

1 one 一	**11** eleven 十一	**21** twenty-one 二十一	**1,000** one thousand 一千
2 two 二	**12** twelve 十二	**30** thirty 三十	**10,000** ten thousand 一萬
3 three 三	**13** thirteen 十三	**40** forty 四十	**100,000** one hundred thousand 十萬
4 four 四	**14** fourteen 十四	**50** fifty 五十	**1,000,000** one million 一百萬
5 five 五	**15** fifteen 十五	**60** sixty 六十	**+** plus 加
6 six 六	**16** sixteen 十六	**70** seventy 七十	**—** minus 減
7 seven 七	**17** seventeen 十七	**80** eighty 八十	**✕** times 乘
8 eight 八	**18** eighteen 十八	**90** ninety 九十	**÷** divided by 除
9 nine 九	**19** nineteen 十九	**100** one hundred 一百	**＝** equals 等於
10 ten 十	**20** twenty 二十	**101** one hundred and one 一百零一	

¼	⅓	½	¾	1
one quarter/ one fourth 四分之一	one third 三分之一	one half 二分之一	three quarters/ three fourths 四分之三	one 一

first 第一   second 第二   third 第三   fourth 第四

100% one hundred percent 百分之百

10% ten percent 百分之十

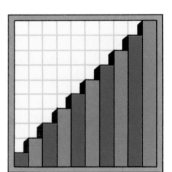

How much is <u>4 + 6</u>? <u>10</u>
How much is <u>4 – 3</u>? <u>1</u>
How much is <u>4 x 4</u>? <u>16</u>
How much is <u>4 ÷ 2</u>? <u>2</u>

How much is 5 + 3? ....
How much is 50 – 15? ....
How much is 13 x 30? ....

How much is 350 ÷ 2? ....
.....................? ....

a. clock　時鐘
b. hour hand　時針
c. minute hand　分針
d. face　鐘面
e. (digital) watch　（數字）手錶
f. (analog) watch　（指針）手錶
g. twelve o'clock/midnight
十二時／午夜
h. twelve o'clock/noon
十二時／中午
i. eight A.M./eight (o'clock)
in the morning　上午八時
j. eight P.M./eight (o'clock)
at night　晚上八時
k. seven o'clock/seven　七時
l. seven o five/five after seven
七時五分
m. seven ten/ten after seven
七時十分
n. seven fifteen/a quarter
after seven　七時十五分
o. seven twenty/twenty
after seven　七時二十分
p. seven twenty-five/
twenty-five after seven
七時二十五分
q. seven thirty/half past seven
七時三十分
r. seven thirty-five/twenty-five
to eight　七時三十五分
s. seven forty/twenty to eight
七時四十分
t. seven forty-five/a quarter to eight
七時四十五分
u. seven fifty/ten to eight
七時五十分
v. seven fifty-five/five to eight
七時五十五分

What time is it? .
It's <u>seven o'clock</u>.

What time is it?
It's ....

What time is it?
It's ....

.................?
....

A 1990

A. Year 年

B. Months 月

January 一月
February 二月
March 三月
April 四月
May 五月
June 六月
July 七月
August 八月
September 九月
October 十月
November 十一月
December 十二月

C. Days of the Week
一週中的日子

S Sunday 星期日
M Monday 星期一
T Tuesday 星期二
W Wednesday 星期三
T Thursday 星期四
F Friday 星期五
S Saturday 星期六

D. Holidays 假日

1. New Year's Day 元旦
2. Valentine's Day 情人節
3. Washington's Birthday 華盛頓誕辰日
4. St. Patrick's Day 聖帕特里克日
5. Easter 復活節
6. Mother's Day 母親節
7. Memorial Day 陣亡將士紀念日
8. Father's Day 父親節
9. Fourth of July/ Independence Day 美國獨立紀念日
10. Labour Day 勞工節
11. Halloween 萬聖節前夕
12. Thanksgiving 感恩節
13. Christmas 聖誕節

B JANUARY
S	M	T	W	T	F	S
	1	2	3	4	5	6
7	8	9	10	11	12	13
14	15	16	17	18	19	20
21	22	23	24	25	26	27
28	29	30	31			

FEBRUARY
S	M	T	W	T	F	S
				1	2	3
4	5	6	7	8	9	10
11	12	13	14	15	16	17
18	19	20	21	22	23	24
25	26	27	28			

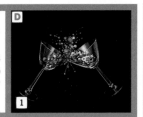

MARCH
S	M	T	W	T	F	S
				1	2	3
4	5	6	7	8	9	10
11	12	13	14	15	16	17
18	19	20	21	22	23	24
25	26	27	28	29	30	31

APRIL
S	M	T	W	T	F	S
1	2	3	4	5	6	7
8	9	10	11	12	13	14
15	16	17	18	19	20	21
22	23	24	25	26	27	28
29	30					

MAY
S	M	T	W	T	F	S
		1	2	3	4	5
6	7	8	9	10	11	12
13	14	15	16	17	18	19
20	21	22	23	24	25	26
27	28	29	30	31		

JUNE
S	M	T	W	T	F	S
					1	2
3	4	5	6	7	8	9
10	11	12	13	14	15	16
17	18	19	20	21	22	23
24	25	26	27	28	29	30

JULY
S	M	T	W	T	F	S
1	2	3	4	5	6	7
8	9	10	11	12	13	14
15	16	17	18	19	20	21
22	23	24	25	26	27	28
29	30	31				

AUGUST
S	M	T	W	T	F	S
			1	2	3	4
5	6	7	8	9	10	11
12	13	14	15	16	17	18
19	20	21	22	23	24	25
26	27	28	29	30	31	

No Holiday

SEPTEMBER
S	M	T	W	T	F	S
						1
2	3	4	5	6	7	8
9	10	11	12	13	14	15
16	17	18	19	20	21	22
23	24	25	26	27	28	29
30						

OCTOBER
S	M	T	W	T	F	S
	1	2	3	4	5	6
7	8	9	10	11	12	13
14	15	16	17	18	19	20
21	22	23	24	25	26	27
28	29	30	31			

NOVEMBER
S	M	T	W	T	F	S
				1	2	3
4	5	6	7	8	9	10
11	12	13	14	15	16	17
18	19	20	21	22	23	24
25	26	27	28	29	30	

DECEMBER
S	M	T	W	T	F	S
						1
2	3	4	5	6	7	8
9	10	11	12	13	14	15
16	17	18	19	20	21	22
23	24	25	26	27	28	29
30	31					

When is Easter?
It's on April 15th.

When is Mother's Day?
It's on ....

When is Halloween?
It's on ....

WEATHER & SEASONS
天氣及季節

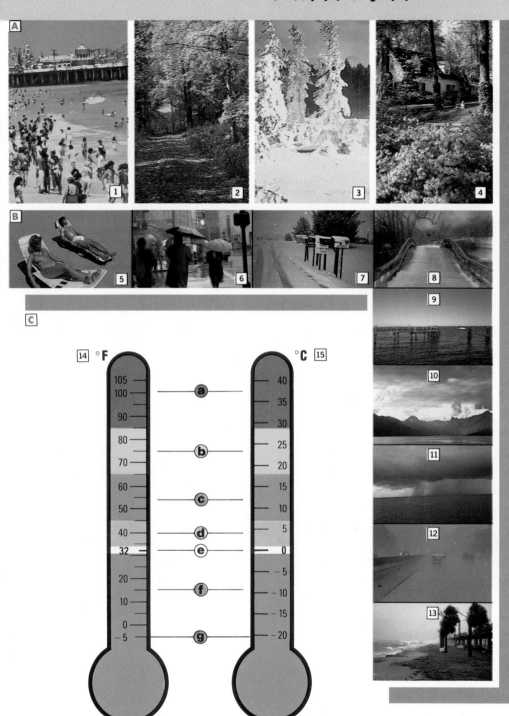

A. Seasons 季節
1. summer　夏季
2. fall　秋季
3. winter　冬季
4. spring　春季

B. Weather 天氣
5. sunny　晴
6. rainy　雨
7. snowy　有雪
8. icy　冰冷
9. clear　晴朗無雲
10. cloudy　多雲
11. stormy　暴風雨
12. foggy　多霧
13. windy　大風

C. Temperature
氣溫
14. degrees Fahrenheit　華氏度數
15. degrees Celsius/
    degrees Centigrade　攝氏度數
a. hot　熱
b. warm　暖
c. cool/chilly　涼／冷
d. cold　寒冷
e. freezing　冰冷
f. below freezing　冰點以下
g. five (degrees) below
   (zero)/minus twenty
   (degrees)
   華氏零下五度 ／
   攝氏負二十度

Is it hot out?
Yes, it's 90°./No, it's 75°.

Is it cold out?
Yes, it's ....

Is it warm out?
No, it's ....

Is it freezing out?
Yes, it's ....

Is it cool out?
No, it's ....

SHAPES 形狀

A. Cube 立方體
1. corner 角
2. top 頂
3. front 前面
4. edge 邊緣
5. depth 深度
6. height 高度

B. Isosceles Triangle
等邊三角形
7. obtuse angle 鈍角
8. acute angle 銳角

C. Right Triangle
直角三角形
9. apex 頂點
10. hypotenuse 斜邊
11. base 底邊
12. right angle 直角

D. Square 方形
13. side 邊

E. Rectangle
長方形
14. width 闊度
15. length 長度
16. diagonal 對角線

F. Circle 圓
17. circumference 圓周
18. center 圓心
19. diameter 直徑
20. radius 半徑

G. Oval/Ellipse
橢圓形

H. Cylinder
圓柱體

I. Sphere 球體

J. Lines 線
21. perpendicular 垂直
22. parallel 平行
23. spiral 螺旋

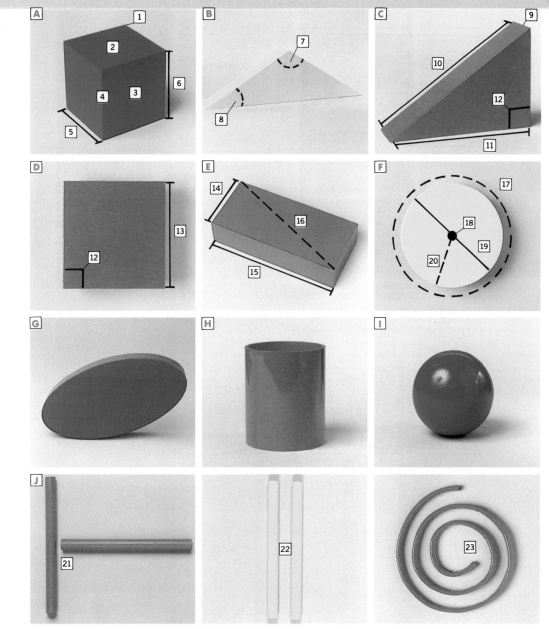

What color is the square?
It's <u>red</u>.

What color is ....?
It's ....

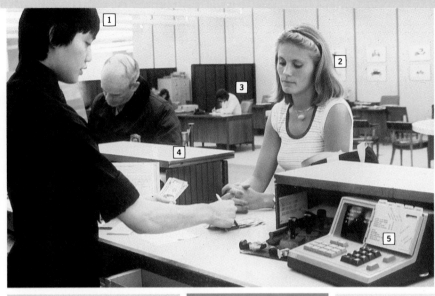

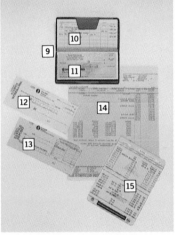

1. teller　出納
2. customer　顧客
3. bank officer銀行職員
4. counter　櫃枱
5. computer　電腦
6. bank vault　銀行保險庫
7. safe deposit vault　保險箱
8. cash machine/
   automatic teller自動提款機
9. checkbook　支票簿
10. check register/
    record　支票登記簿
11. check　支票
12. withdrawal slip　提款單
13. deposit slip　存款單
14. monthly statement
    月報表／月結單
15. bank book　銀行存摺
16. traveler's check　旅行支票
17. credit card　信用卡
18. money order　滙票
19. penny　一分
20. nickel　五分鎳幣

21. dime　一角銀幣
22. quarter　二角五分銀幣
23. half dollar/fifty
    cent piece　五角銀幣
24. silver dollar　一美元銀幣
25. dollar (bill)/
    one dollar　一美元鈔票
26. five (dollar bill)/
    five dollars　五美元鈔票
27. ten (dollar bill)/
    ten dollars　十美元鈔票
28. twenty (dollar bill)/
    twenty dollars
    二十美元鈔票
29. fifty (dollar bill)/
    fifty dollars
    五十美元鈔票
30. one hundred
    (dollar bill)/one
    hundred dollars
    一百美元鈔票

Do you have change
for a <u>ten</u>?
Sure. Here are two <u>fives</u>.

Do you have change
for a ....?
Sure. Here are four ....

Do you have change
for a ....?
Sure. Here are two .... and a ....

THE WORLD 世界

Arctic Ocean

Greenland

Baffin Bay

Greenland Sea

United States

Canada

Iceland

Hudson Bay

United States

Atlantic

Pacific

Gulf of Mexico

Bahamas

Mexico

Haiti

Cuba

Dominican Republic

Belize

Jamaica

Puerto Rico

Caribbean Sea

Ocean

Guatemala

El Salvador

Honduras

Nicaragua

Costa Rica

Panama

Venezuela

Guyana

Suriname

French Guiana

Colombia

Ecuador

Peru

Brazil

Ocean

Bolivia

Paraguay

Chile

Uruguay

Argentina

Falkland Islands

Antarctica

North America
北美洲

South America
南美洲

Europe 歐洲

Asia 亞洲

Africa 非洲

Australia 澳洲

Antarctica
南極洲

| Where's Paraguay? | Where's France? | Where's Japan? | ....? |
| It's in South America. | It's in .... | It's in .... | .... |

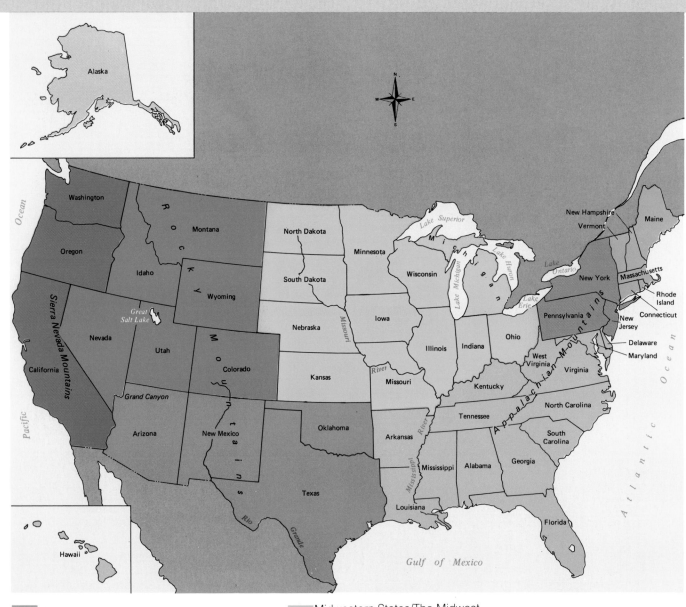

New England/The East 新英格蘭／東部	Midwestern States/The Midwest 中西部各州／中西部	**N** north 北
Middle Atlantic States/The East 大西洋中部各州／東部	Rocky Mountain States 落磯山各州	**S** south 南
Southern States/The South 南部各州／南部	Pacific Coast States/The West Coast 太平洋沿岸各州／西海岸	**E** east 東
Southwestern States/The Southwest 西南部各州／西南部		**W** west 西

Is Utah <u>north of</u> Arizona?
Yes, it is.

Is Utah <u>east of</u> Colorado?
No, it isn't. It's <u>west of</u> Colorado.

Is California south of Oregon? ....?
....

Is Missouri east of Kansas?
....

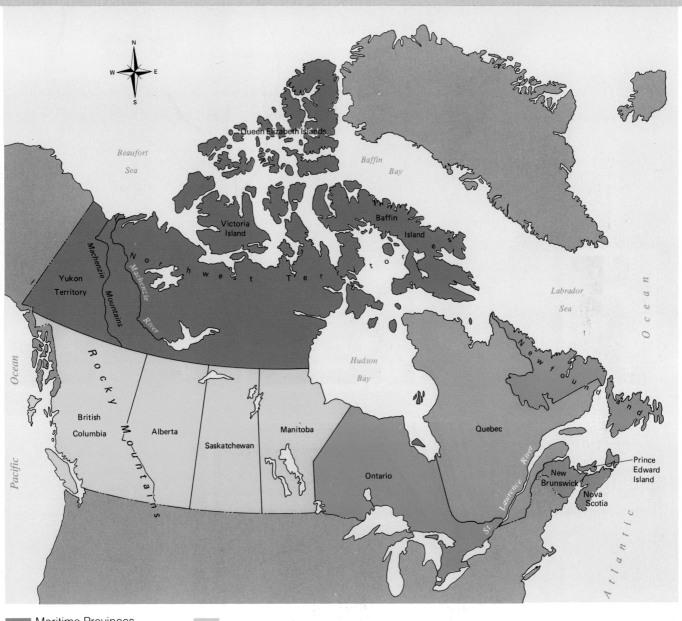

Maritime Provinces
沿海各省

Western Canada 加拿大西部

Quebec 魁北克

Northern Canada 加拿大北部

Ontario 安大略

Is Ontario <u>west of</u> Quebec?
Yes, it is.

Is British Columbia <u>north of</u> Alberta?
No, it isn't. It's <u>west of</u> Alberta.

Is Newfoundland south of New Brunswick?
....

Is Manitoba east of Saskatchewan?
....

1. skyline　大都市面貌
2. skyscraper　摩天大樓
3. fire hydrant　消防栓
4. trash can　垃圾箱
5. parking lot　停車場
6. parking meter
   停車碼錶／泊車咪錶
7. traffic light　交通燈
8. flag　旗
9. street　街道
10. crosswalk
    行人穿越道／行人橫道
11. pedestrian　行人
12. bus lane　巴士專線
13. (street) corner　街角
14. curb　路邊石
15. phone booth/telephone
    booth　電話亭
16. walk sign　行人指示燈
17. one way (traffic) sign
    單程路牌／單行道標誌
18. office building　辦公大樓

19. traffic (jam) 交通（堵塞）
20. subway (entrance)
   地下鐵道（入口）
21. newsstand 報攤
22. street light 路燈
23. bus stop 巴士站
24. street sign 街名牌
25. bus 巴士
26. exit 出口
27. passenger 乘客
28. sidewalk 人行道

5 Is there a <u>parking lot</u> near here?
Yes, there is./No, there isn't.

15 Is there a .... near here?   23 Is there a .... near here?   21 ....?   20 ....?
....

A. Check-out Area
付款處

1. customer/shopper 顧客
2. cashier 出納
3. cash register 收款機
4. checkbook 支票簿
5. groceries 食品雜貨
6. packer 包裝員
7. bag/sack 袋子
8. check-out counter 付賬櫃枱

B. Frozen Foods
冷凍食品

9. frozen vegetables 冷凍蔬菜
10. frozen dinner 冷凍晚餐
11. frozen orange juice 冷凍橙汁

C. Dairy 奶製品

12. yogurt 酸乳酪
13. cheese 乾酪
14. eggs 蛋類
15. margarine
人造牛油（香港）／奶油（台灣
16. butter 牛油（香港）／奶油（台灣
17. milk 牛奶

D. Canned Goods
罐裝食品

18. tuna fish　金槍魚／鮪魚
19. soup　湯

E. Meat and Poultry
肉及家禽

20. bacon　烟肉（香港）／培根（台灣）
21. roast　烤肉
22. pork chops　猪排
23. chicken/roaster　雞
24. ground meat　碎肉
25. steak　牛排
26. lamb chops　羊排

F. Packaged Goods
包裝食品

27. bread　麵包
28. cereal　穀類食物／玉米片
29. cookies　小甜餅／曲奇餅
30. crackers　薄脆餅乾
31. macaroni　通心粉

19 I need a can of <u>soup</u>.
28 I need a box of <u>cereal</u>.
20 I need a pound of <u>bacon</u>.
17 I need a carton of <u>milk</u>.

18 I need a can of ....
31 I need a box of ....
24 I need a pound of ....
14 I need a carton of ....

FRUIT 水果

1. apples　蘋果
2. pears　梨
3. grapes　葡萄
4. kiwis　獼猴桃／奇異果
5. mangoes　芒果
6. coconuts　椰子
7. avocados
   鱷梨／牛油果
8. bananas　香蕉
9. nectarines　油桃／桃駁李
10. plums　梅子／李子
11. cherries　櫻桃
12. apricots　杏
13. lemons　檸檬
14. limes　青檸檬
15. grapefruit　西柚／葡萄柚
16. oranges　橙／橘子
17. pineapples　菠蘿／鳳梨
18. papayas　木瓜
19. peaches　桃子
20. strawberries　草莓
21. raspberries　蔗莓
22. blueberries　藍莓
23. watermelons　西瓜
24. honeydew melons　（哈）蜜
25. cantaloupes　皺皮（哈）蜜

Do you need any apples? Yes, I need <u>some</u>./No, we don't need <u>any</u>.

Do you need any cherries?　　　Do you need any grapes?　　　..........?

....　　　　　　　　　　..........　　　　　　　　　　..........

VEGETABLES 蔬菜

1. lettuce 萵苣／生菜
2. green onions/ scallions 葱
3. radishes 小紅蘿蔔
4. watercress 西洋菜（香港） ／水田芥（台灣）
5. tomatoes 西紅柿／番茄
6. cucumbers 黃瓜／青瓜
7. celery 芹菜
8. yellow peppers 黃燈籠椒
9. green peppers 青燈籠椒
10. red peppers 紅燈籠椒
11. new potatoes 鮮馬鈴薯
12. baking potatoes 烘焙馬鈴薯
13. sweet potatoes 白薯／番薯
14. onions 洋葱
15. red onions 紅葱頭
16. pearl onions 小洋葱頭

17. cauliflower 菜花
18. spinach 菠菜
19. garlic 大蒜／蒜頭
20. artichokes 朝鮮薊
21. green beans/ string beans 扁豆
22. eggplants 茄子／矮瓜
23. carrots 胡蘿蔔
24. asparagus 蘆筍／露筍
25. broccoli 西蘭花
26. corn 玉米／栗米
27. ginger 薑
28. parsnips 防風草根
29. cabbage 包心菜／椰菜（香港）
30. leeks 大葱
31. turnips 蘿蔔
32. dill 蒔蘿

14 I'd like a pound of <u>onions</u>.
7 I'd like a bunch of <u>celery</u>.
1 I'd like a head of <u>lettuce</u>.

5 I'd like a pound of ....
32 I'd like a bunch of ....
29 I'd like a head of ....

THE MENU 菜單

A. Appetizers 開胃菜

1. tomato juice　番茄汁
2. fruit cup/fruit cocktail　什錦水果
3. shrimp cocktail　蝦拼盤

B. Soup and Salad 湯與沙律／沙拉

4. soup　湯
5. (tossed) salad　（拌）沙律／（拌）沙拉

C. Main Courses/Entrées 主餐／正菜

6. steak　牛排
7. baked potato　烤馬鈴薯/烤薯仔
8. (dinner) roll　（晚餐）圓麵包
9. roast beef　烤牛肉
10. stuffed tomatoes　釀番茄/釀西紅柿
11. pork chops　猪排
12. carrots　胡蘿蔔
13. spaghetti and meatballs　肉丸意大利粉／麵條
14. roast chicken　烤雞
15. green beans　扁豆
16. peaches　桃
17. fish　魚
18. broccoli　西蘭花

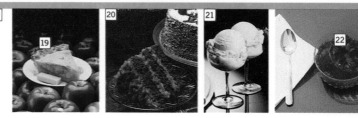

D. Desserts 餐後甜品／甜點

19. apple pie　蘋果（餡）餅
20. chocolate cake　巧克力／朱古力蛋糕
21. ice cream　冰淇淋／雪糕
22. jello　果子凍／啫喱

E. Beverages 飲料

23. coffee　咖啡
24. tea　茶

Would you like <u>tea</u> or <u>coffee</u>?
I'd like <u>tea</u>./I'd like <u>coffee</u>.

Would you like soup or salad?
I'd like ....

Would you like .... or ....?
....

FAST FOODS & SNACKS
快餐與小吃

1. hero/submarine sandwich
大型三明治／三文治
2. roast beef sandwich
烤牛肉三明治／三文治
3. pizza 意大利肉餅／薄餅
4. fried clams 炸蛤
5. fried chicken 炸雞
6. mustard 芥末
7. ketchup 番茄醬

8. relish 開胃小菜
9. pickles 泡菜
10. onions 洋葱
11. potato chips 炸薯片
12. tortilla chips 炸玉米片
13. pretzels 椒鹽脆餅條
14. popcorn 玉米花／爆谷
15. peanuts 花生

16. candy bar/chocolate
巧克力／朱古力
17. (chewing) gum
口香糖／香口膠
18. donut 炸餅圈／甜甜圈
19. milk shake 奶昔
20. soft drink/soda 汽水
21. straw 吸管

22. (paper) napkin
紙餐巾
23. (paper) plate 紙碟
24. hamburger
漢堡飽／漢堡
25. hot dog 熱狗
26. onion rings 炸洋葱圈
27. french fries 炸薯條

25 Do you like <u>hot dogs</u>?	Yes, I do./No, I don't.
9 Do you like <u>pickles</u>?	Yes, I do./No, I don't.

27 Do you like ....? ....
13 Do you like ....? ....

11 ....? ....
15 ....? ....

1. postal clerk　郵局職員
2. package/parcel　包裹
3. scale　磅／秤
4. express mail　快郵
5. mail slot　信箱入信口
6. mail truck　郵車
7. mail carrier　郵差
8. mailbag　郵袋
9. mailbox　郵筒／郵箱
10. stamp machine
　　自動售郵票機
11. sheet of stamps
　　郵票印張
12. roll of stamps　卷裝郵票
13. book of stamps　簿裝郵票
14. envelope　信封
15. return address　回郵地址
16. address　地址
17. zip code　郵遞區號碼
18. stamp　郵票
19. (picture) postcard　明信片
20. return receipt　回執
21. certified mail　登記信
　　（負責寄到，要求收信人
　　簽收，但不補償損失）

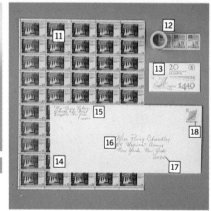

What's Dale Harvey's address?
<u>828 Chauncey Street. Baltimore, Maryland.</u>

What's his zip code?
<u>21217.</u>

What's your address?
....

What's your zip code?
....

THE OFFICE 辦公室

1. secretary 秘書
2. (desk) lamp 枱燈
3. index file/Rolodex
索引查閱機
4. pencil holder 鉛筆筒
5. (electric) pencil sharpener
（電動）鉛筆鉋（機）
6. typewriter 打字機
7. typing paper 打字紙
8. tape dispenser 膠紙座架
9. tape/Scotch tape 膠紙／膠帶
10. stapler 釘書機
11. in box 來件格
12. out box 出件格
13. paper clip holder 紙夾盒
14. stationery 文具
15. wastepaper basket 廢紙簍
16. file cabinet 文件櫃／檔案櫃
17. file folder 文件夾
18. bulletin board
告示牌／佈告牌
19. receptionist 接待員
20. telephone/switchboard
電話／電話總機
21. note pad 便箋
22. message pad 留言本
23. desk calendar 桌曆／枱日曆
24. desk 辦公桌
25. (ball point) pen 原子筆
26. pencil 鉛筆
27. eraser 橡皮擦
28. rubber band 橡皮筋
29. paper clip 紙夾
30. staple 釘書釘
31. photocopier/Xerox
machine 影印機

Where's the stapler?	It's <u>on</u> the desk.
Where's the typing paper?	It's <u>in</u> the typewriter.
Where's the pencil sharpener?	It's <u>next to</u> the pencil holder.

Where's the in box?   It's .... the desk.
Where's the paper clip?   It's .... the proper clip holder.
Where's the tape dispenser?   It's .... the stapler.
Where's the wastepaper basket?   It's .... the desk.

1. construction worker
   建築工人
2. bricklayer/mason
   砌磚工／泥水匠
3. carpenter 木匠
4. painter 油漆工
5. window washer
   抹窗工人
6. sanitation worker 清潔工
7. truck driver 卡車司機
8. mechanic 機工／技工
9. welder 電焊工
10. electrician 電工
11. plumber 鉛管工
12. firefighter 消防員
13. police officer 警察
14. mail carrier 郵差
15. fisherman 漁民
16. farmer 農民
17. florist 花店主
18. grocer 食品雜貨商
19. butcher 屠夫
20. baker 麵包師傅
21. chef/cook 廚師
22. waiter 男服務生／侍應
23. waitress 女服務生／侍應

24. scientist　科學家
25. doctor/pediatrician
　　醫生／兒科醫生
26. nurse　護士
27. dentist　牙科醫生
28. (dental) hygienist
　　（牙科）衛生學家
29. optometrist　驗光配鏡師
30. veterinarian　獸醫
31. pharmacist　藥劑師
32. newscaster　新聞廣播員
33. journalist　記者
34. computer technician
　　電腦技術員
35. teacher　教師
36. architect　建築師
37. secretary　秘書
38. teller　銀行出納
39. salesperson　售貨員
40. hairdresser　美容師
41. barber　理髮師
42. tailor　裁縫
43. seamstress　女縫紉工
44. model　模特兒
45. photographer　攝影師
46. artist　畫家

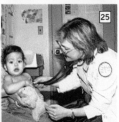

Would you like to be a <u>carpenter</u>?
Yes, I would./No, I wouldn't. I'd rather
be a <u>painter</u>.

Would you like to be a ....?
....
Would you like to be a ....?
....

..........?
....

THE BODY 軀體

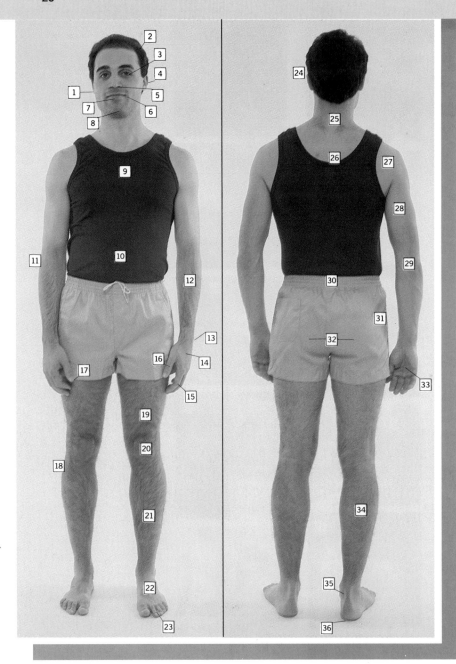

1. face 臉
2. hair 頭髮
3. eye 眼睛
4. ear 耳朵
5. nose 鼻
6. mouth 口
7. lip 嘴唇
8. chin 下巴
9. chest 胸
10. stomach 腹/肚
11. arm 臂
12. forearm 前臂
13. wrist 腕
14. hand 手
15. finger 手指
16. thumb 拇指
17. nail 指甲
18. leg 腿
19. thigh 大腿
20. knee 膝
21. shin 脛骨
22. foot 腳
23. toe 腳趾
24. head 頭
25. neck 頸
26. back 背
27. shoulder 肩
28. upper arm 上臂
29. elbow 手肘
30. waist 腰
31. hip 股
32. buttocks 臀
33. palm 手掌
34. calf 小腿
35. ankle 足踝
36. heel 踵／後跟

37. blonde 金髮女人
38. brunette 深色頭髮女人
39. redhead 紅頭髮的人
40. forehead 額
41. temple 太陽穴
42. eyebrow 眉毛
43. eyelid 眼瞼／眼皮
44. eyelash 睫毛
45. pupil 瞳孔
46. cheek 面頰
47. mustache 鬍子
48. tooth 牙齒
49. beard 鬚

50. tongue 舌
51. brain 腦
52. artery 動脈
53. vein 靜脈
54. throat 咽喉
55. lung 肺
56. heart 心臟／心
57. liver 肝臟
58. gall bladder 膽囊
59. small intestine 小腸
60. large intestine 大腸
61. fatty tissue 脂肪組織

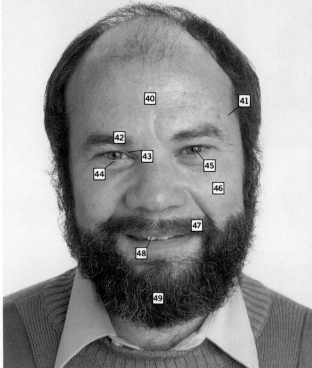

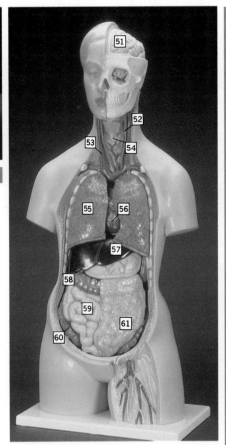

What's that called? 59 The small intestine.

What's that called?   57 The ....
What's that called?   60 The ....
..........?   56 ....
..........?   51 ....

COSMETICS & TOILETRIES
化妝品及化妝用具

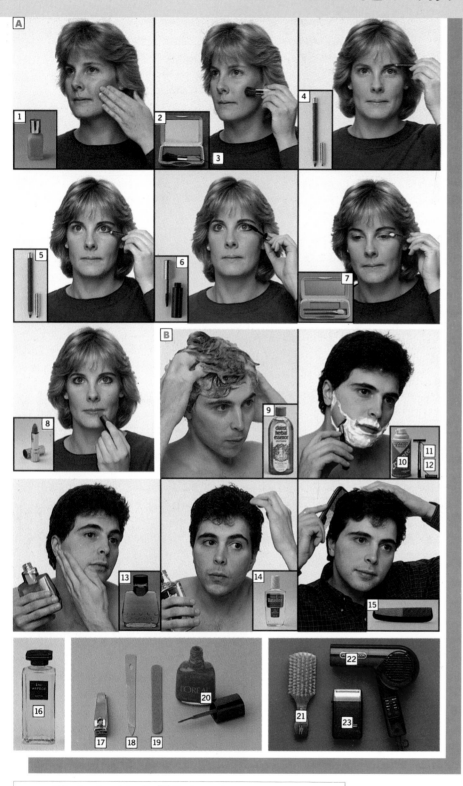

A. Cosmetics
化妝品
1. base/foundation 粉底
2. blush/rouge 胭脂
3. brush 刷子
4. eyebrow pencil 眉筆
5. eyeliner 眼線筆
6. mascara 睫毛液
7. eye shadow 眼影
8. lipstick 唇膏／口紅

B. Toiletries
化妝用具
9. shampoo 洗髮水（精）
10. shaving cream 刮鬍膏
11. razor 刮鬍刀
12. razor blade 刀片
13. after-shave (lotion) 鬍後水／刮鬍水
14. hair tonic 生髮水
15. comb 梳
16. cologne 古龍水／花露水
17. nail clipper 指甲鉗
18. nail file 指甲銼
19. emery board 砂板
20. nail polish 指甲油
21. (hair) brush 髮刷
22. hair dryer 吹風器
23. electric shaver 電刮鬍刀

What's she doing?	8 She's putting on <u>lipstick</u>.	
What's he doing?	13 He's putting on <u>after-shave</u>.	

What's she doing?　　6 She's putting on ....? 　7 ....
What's he doing?　　14 He's putting on ....? 　2 ....

5. brush your teeth 刷牙
6. shave 刮臉
7. get dressed 穿衣

1. wake up 醒來
2. get up 起床
3. take a shower 淋浴
4. dry off 抹乾

8. wash your face 洗臉
9. rinse your face 沖臉
10. put on makeup 化粧
11. brush your hair 刷頭髮

12. cook 煮
13. eat 吃
14. drink 飲／喝
15. sweep 掃地
16. dust 抹
17. watch (TV) 看（電視）
18. listen 聽

19. take a bath 洗澡
20. comb your hair 梳頭髮
21. go to bed 上床
22. sleep 睡覺

What does he do everyday?	[2] He <u>gets</u> up.
What does she do everyday?	[8] She <u>washes</u> her face.
What does she do everyday?	[21] She <u>goes</u> to bed.

What does she do everyday?   [20] She .... her hair.
What does he do everyday?   [5] He .... his teeth.
..........?   [6] ....

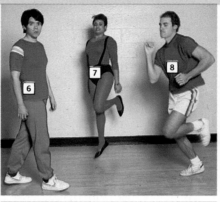
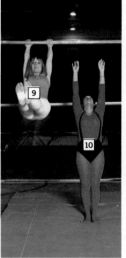

1. bend 屈身	5. kneel 跪	9. swing 擺動	13. push 推
2. stretch 伸展	6. walk 行走	10. reach 伸手／抓	14. lift 舉起
3. sit 坐	7. hop 單足跳	11. catch 接（球）	15. pull 拉
4. lie down 躺下	8. run 跑	12. throw 擲（球）	16. kick 踢

What's he doing? [2] He's <u>stretching</u>.
What she doing? [7] She's <u>hopping</u>.

What's he doing? [8] He's ....
What's she doing? [5] She's ....
..........? [1] ....
..........? [9] ....

ACTION AT SCHOOL
學校內的動作

1. write 寫	13. draw 畫
2. teach 教	14. smile 微笑
3. erase 擦掉／抹去	15. laugh 大笑
4. give 給	16. point 指
5. take 取／接	17. touch 摸
6. tear up 撕	18. frown 皺眉
7. carry 捧/拿	19. go up 向上走
8. read 讀	20. wave 揮動
9. pick up 撿起	21. stand 站
10. paint 上色	22. go down 向下走
11. sculpt 雕塑	23. fall 跌
12. cut 剪	

What's he doing? 14 He's <u>smiling</u>.
What's she doing? 18 She's <u>frowning</u>.

What's he doing? 13 He's ....
What's she doing? 10 She's ....
..........? 8 ....
..........? 11 ....

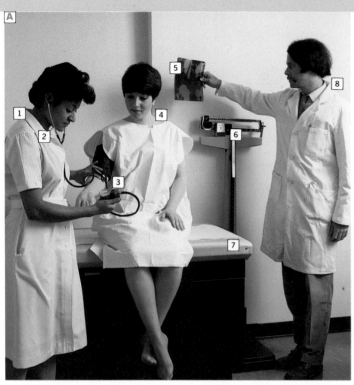

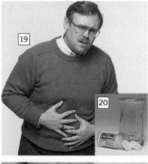

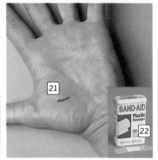

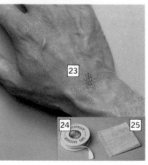

A. The Doctor's Office
診所

1. nurse 護士
2. stethoscope 聽診器
3. blood pressure gauge 血壓計
4. patient 病人
5. x-ray X光
6. scale 體重檢查磅
7. examination table 體檢枱
8. doctor 醫生

B. Sickness and Medicine
疾病及藥

9. headache 頭痛
10. aspirin 阿司匹靈
11. fever 發燒
12. thermometer
    體溫計／寒暑表
13. cold 感冒／傷風
14. tissue/Kleenex 紙巾／面紙

15. cold tablets 感冒藥片
16. cough 咳嗽
17. cough syrup 止咳糖漿
18. cough drops 止咳藥片
19. stomachache 胃痛／肚子痛
20. antacid/Alka Seltzer
    抗酸劑

21. cut 割傷
22. Band-Aid 藥水膠布
23. scratch 抓傷
24. Adhesive tape 膠布
25. bandage/gauze
    繃帶／紗布
26. prescription 藥方

> What do you do for a <u>headache</u>?
> Take <u>aspirin</u>.

What do you do for a ....?
Take Alka Seltzer.

What do you do for a ....?
Take cough drops.

What do you do for a ....?
Take cold tablets.

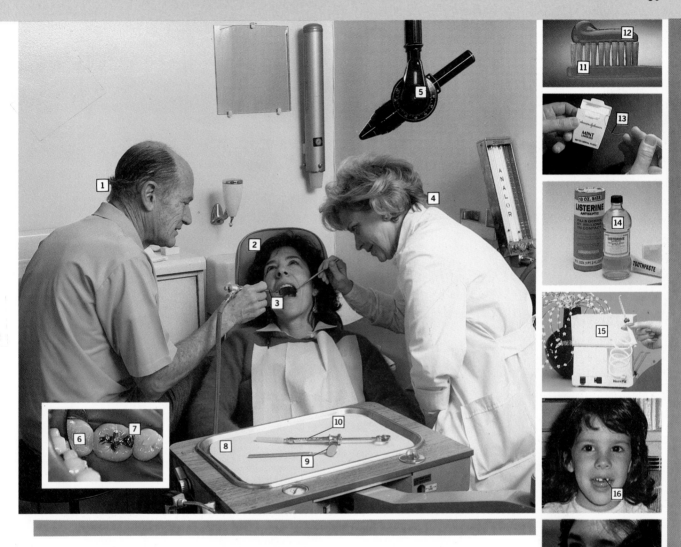

1. dentist 牙醫
2. patient 病人
3. drill 鑽子
4. dental assistant 牙醫助手
5. x-ray machine X光機
6. tooth 牙齒
7. filling 填料
8. tray 托盤
9. mirror 鏡
10. Novocain 麻醉劑
11. toothbrush 牙刷
12. toothpaste 牙膏
13. dental floss 潔齒線
14. mouthwash 漱口水
15. Water Pik 沖洗管
16. missing tooth 缺牙
17. braces 牙齒矯正鋼絲套

16 Have you ever had a <u>missing tooth</u>?
　　Yes, I have./No, I haven't.

7 Have you ever had a ....?
....

17 Have you ever had an ....?
....

Have you ever had ....?
....

THE FAMILY 家庭

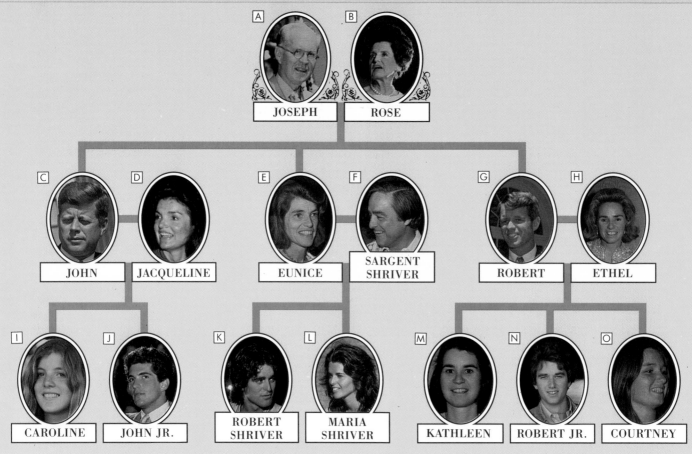

The Kennedy Family 甘迺廸家族

A & B husband and wife 丈夫與妻子
A & C father and son 父與子
A & E father and daughter 父與女
B & C mother and son 母與子
B & E mother and daughter 母與女
C & E brother and sister 兄／弟與姐／妹
C & G brothers 兄弟
M & O sisters 姐妹
C & H brother-in-law and sister-in-law 二伯與弟媳
C & F brothers-in-law 內兄與妹夫／連襟
E & H sisters-in-law 姑與嫂
A & F father-in-law and son-in-law 岳父與女婿
A & H father-in-law and daughter-in-law 公公與兒媳婦

B & F mother-in-law and son-in-law 岳母與女婿
B & H mother-in-law and daughter-in-law 婆婆與兒媳婦
AB & CEG parents and children 父母與子女
AB & IJ grandparents and grandchildren 祖父母與孫子女
A & J grandfather and grandson 祖父與孫子
A & I grandfather and granddaughter 祖父與孫女
B & J grandmother and grandson 祖母與孫子
B & I grandmother and granddaughter 祖母與孫女
C & K uncle and nephew 舅父與外甥
C & L uncle and niece 舅父與外甥女
D & K aunt and nephew 舅母與外甥
D & L aunt and niece 舅母與外甥女
IJ／MNO & KL cousins 表兄弟姐妹／堂兄弟姐妹

Rose is Joseph's <u>wife</u>.
John is Joseph's <u>son</u>.

Rose is John's ....
Caroline is Jacqueline's ....

John is Caroline's ....
....

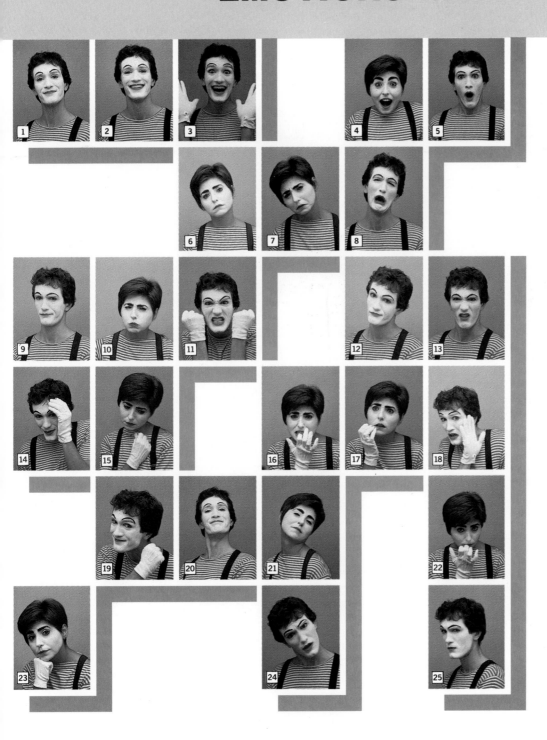

1. pleased 喜悅
2. happy 高興
3. ecstatic 狂喜
4. surprised 驚奇
5. shocked 震驚
6. sad 憂愁
7. miserable 悲慘
8. grieving 哀傷
9. displeased 不高興
10. angry/mad 憤怒
11. furious 狂怒
12. annoyed 懊惱
13. disgusted 厭惡
14. embarrassed 尷尬
15. ashamed 慚愧
16. nervous 緊張不安
17. worried 擔心
18. scared/afraid 受驚
19. determined 堅決
20. proud 驕傲
21. smug 沾沾自喜
22. shy 羞怯
23. bored 厭煩
24. confused 迷惑
25. suspicious 懷疑

Is he <u>happy</u>? [2] Yes, he is.
Is she <u>happy</u>? [6] No, she isn't. She's <u>sad</u>.

Is he pleased?   [1] ....   Is he worried?   [11] ....
Is she angry?   [16] ....   Is she bored?   [23] ....

OPPOSITES 相反詞

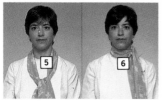

1. neat 整齊
2. messy 雜亂

3. high 高
4. low 低

5. loose 鬆
6. tight 緊

7. light 輕
8. heavy 重

9. long 長
10. short 短

11. good 好
12. bad 壞

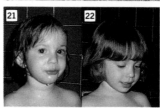

13. tall 高
14. short 矮

15. young 少
16. old 老

17. clean 乾淨
18. dirty 骯髒

19. pretty 美
20. ugly 醜

21. wet 濕
22. dry 乾

23. straight 平直
24. curly 捲曲

25. fast 快
26. slow 慢

27. hot 熱
28. cold 冷

29. open 打開
30. closed 關閉

31. full 滿
32. empty 空

33. new 新
34. old 舊

35. light 光亮
36. dark 黑暗

37. straight 直
38. crooked 曲

39. wide 寬
40. narrow 窄

41. thick 粗
42. thin 細

43. soft 軟
44. hard 硬

45. smooth 光滑
46. rough 粗糙

47. over 在上
48. under 在下

Is it <u>hot</u> or <u>cold</u>?	27 It's <u>hot</u>.
Is she <u>wet</u> or <u>dry</u>?	22 She's <u>dry</u>.

It is neat or messy? 1 It's ....
Is she clean or dirty? 18 She's ....
Is it straight or crooked? 38 ....
Is she young or old? 16 ....
....

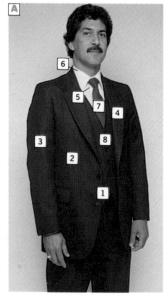

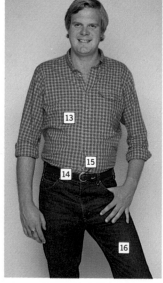

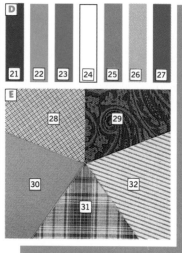

A. The Suit 套裝

1. suit 套裝／一套衣服
2. jacket 上衣／上身
3. sleeve 袖
4. lapel 翻領
5. shirt 襯衣／恤衫
6. collar 衣領
7. tie 領帶
8. vest 背心

B. Casual Wear 便服

9. sport jacket/sport coat 便裝上身／青年裝上衣
10. pocket 口袋
11. sweater 毛衣
12. slacks/pants 褲子
13. sport shirt 花襯衫
14. belt 腰帶
15. (belt) buckle 皮帶扣（環）
16. jeans 牛仔褲

C. Underwear 內衣

17. boxer shorts 短褲
18. briefs/Jockey shorts 內褲／三角褲
19. sock 短襪
20. undershirt/t-shirt 內衣／汗衫

D. Colors 顏色

21. brown 棕
22. gray 灰
23. green 綠
24. white 白
25. red 紅
26. tan 黃褐
27. blue 藍

E. Patterns 圖案

28. checked 方格子
29. paisley 渦旋形圖案
30. solid 純色
31. plaid 格子花呢
32. striped 條紋

22	Do you have a <u>gray</u> suit?	Yes, I do./No, I don't.
7	Do you have a green <u>tie</u>?	Yes, I do./No, I don't.

21 Do you have a .... suit? ....
30 Do you have a .... sweater? ....

9 Do you have a blue ....? ....
5 Do you have a striped ....? ....

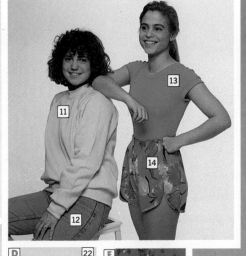

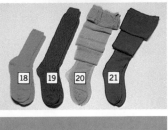

A. The Suit and Dress
套裝與連衣裙

1. suit 套裝
2. jacket 外套
3. skirt 裙子
4. blouse 女襯衣
5. handbag 女用手提包
6. dress 連衣裙 / 洋裝
7. clutch bag 無帶手提包

B. Casual Wear 便服

8. blazer 便服上身
9. slacks/pants 鬆身褲 / 褲
10. shoulder bag 掛包
11. sweatshirt 圓領運動衫
12. jeans 牛仔褲
13. t-shirt 運動衫/ T 恤
14. shorts 短褲

C. Underwear 內衣

15. (half) slip 底 / 襯裙
16. bra 乳罩
17. underpants/panties 內褲
18. sock 短襪
19. knee sock 中統襪
20. panty hose 絲褲襪
21. tights 緊身褲

D. Colors 顏色

22. pink 粉紅
23. yellow 黃
24. purple 紫
25. orange 橙
26. turquoise 天藍
27. black 黑
28. beige 米色

E. Patterns 圖案

29. print 印花布
30. flowered 花形圖案
31. polka dot 圓點

| What's she wearing? | 11 She's wearing a <u>yellow sweatshirt</u>. |
| What's she wearing? | 14 She's wearing <u>flowered shorts</u>. |

What's she wearing?　13 She's wearing a ....

What's she wearing?　12 She's wearing ....

What's she wearing?　9 She's wearing ....

What's she wearing?　8 She's wearing a ....

A. Outerwear
戶外服裝
1. coat 大衣
2. jacket 夾克
3. cap 鴨舌帽／便帽
4. hat 帽子
5. glove 手套

B. Rainwear
雨天服裝
6. umbrella 雨傘
7. raincoat/trench coat 雨衣
8. rain hat 雨帽

C. Sweaters 毛衣
9. crewneck 圓領
10. turtleneck 翻折高領／樽領
11. V-neck V領
12. cardigan 羊毛外套

D. Footwear 鞋類
13. shoe 鞋
14. heel 鞋跟
15. sole 鞋底
16. shoelace 鞋帶
17. loafer 懶人鞋
18. sneaker 運動鞋
19. sandal 涼鞋
20. slipper 拖鞋
21. boot 靴

E. Nightwear 睡衣
22. robe 睡袍
23. nightgown 女睡衣
24. pajamas 睡衣褲

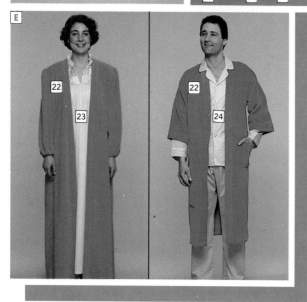

always ● 永遠　often ✖ 經常　rarely ⊙ 極少　never ○ 永遠不

4 Do you ever wear a <u>hat</u>?	Yes, I <u>always</u> wear one.	7 Do you ever wear a ....?	.... wear one.
1 Do you ever wear a <u>coat</u>?	Yes, I <u>often</u> wear one.	10 Do you ever wear a ....?	.... wear one.
3 Do you ever wear a <u>cap</u>?	Yes, I <u>rarely</u> wear one.	12 ....?	....
22 Do you ever wear a <u>robe</u>?	No, I <u>never</u> wear one.	2 ....?	....

ACCESSORIES 飾物及配用品

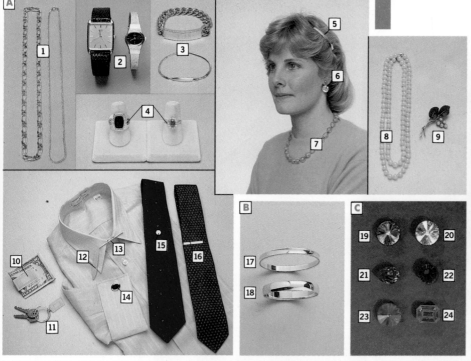

A. Jewelry 首飾
1. chain 鏈
2. watch 手錶
3. bracelet 手鐲
4. ring 戒指
5. barrette 髮夾
6. earring 耳環
7. necklace 項鏈
8. pearls 珍珠
9. pin 胸針
10. money clip 錢夾
11. key ring 鑰匙圈
12. stay 領尖定型簽
13. collar bar 項夾
14. cuff link 袖口鈕／袖扣
15. tiepin/tie tack 領帶別針
16. tie bar/tie clip 別針／領帶夾

B. Metals 金屬
17. gold 金
18. silver 銀

C. Gems 寶石
19. topaz 黃晶／黃寶石
20. diamond 鑽石
21. amethyst 紫晶
22. ruby 紅寶石
23. sapphire 藍寶石
24. emerald 綠寶石

D. Accessories 配用品
25. briefcase 公文皮包
26. tote bag 大手提包
27. attaché case 公文提箱／手提箱
28. change purse 零錢包
29. wallet 皮夾
30. scarf 圍巾
31. handkerchief 手帕

Is that a <u>gold chain</u>?   1   Yes, it is.

Is that a <u>gold bracelet</u>?   3   No, it's not. It's a <u>silver bracelet</u>.

Is that a gold watch?   2 ....   Is that a silver money clip?   10 ....

Is that a silver earring?   6 ....   Is that a gold tiepin?   15 ....

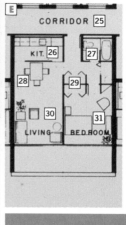

A. Two-Story House 兩層樓房

1. driveway 車道
2. garage door 車房門
3. garage 車房
4. roof 屋頂
5. side door 側門
6. chimney 煙囪
7. gutter 排水溝
8. window 窗
9. shutter 百葉窗
10. (porch) light 門廊燈
11. lawn 草坪

B. Ranch House 平房／單層房屋

12. front walk 屋前小徑
13. doorknob 球形門把手
14. front door 前門

C. Two-Family House/Duplex 兩戶複式住宅

15. antenna 天綫
16. upstairs apartment 樓上住宅
17. downstairs apartment 樓下住宅
18. mailbox 郵箱
19. (front) steps （前）台階

D. Apartment Building 公寓大樓

20. lobby 門廳
21. elevator 電梯
22. first floor 一樓
23. second floor 二樓
24. balcony 陽臺／露臺

E. Floor Plan 樓面設計圖

25. hall/corridor 走廊
26. kitchen 廚房
27. bathroom 浴室
28. dining room 飯廳
29. closet 小櫥
30. living room 客廳
31. bedroom 睡房

Have you ever lived in <u>an apartment building</u>?
Yes, I have./No, I haven't.

Have you ever lived in a two-story house?
....
Have you ever lived in a ranch house?
....

Have you ever lived in a two-family house?
....

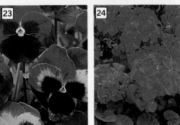

1. tree 樹
2. leaf 樹葉
3. lawn/grass 草坪
4. lawn mower 割草機
5. lounge chair 躺椅
6. wading pool 兒童玩水池
7. barbecue 野餐烤肉架
8. patio 石板涼台
9. umbrella 太陽傘
10. (patio) table 花園桌
11. (patio) chair 花園椅
12. bush 灌木
13. flower bed 花壇

14. hedge 樹籬
15. vegetable garden 菜園
16. watering can 澆水器
17. rake 耙
18. trowel 小鏟子
19. rose 玫瑰
20. daisy 雛菊
21. azalea 杜鵑花
22. snapdragon 金魚草
23. pansy 三色紫羅蘭
24. geranium 天竺葵
25. tulip 鬱金香
26. daffodil 水仙花

Do you like <u>roses</u>?
Yes, I do./No, I don't. I like <u>tulips</u> better.

Do you like daisies?   Do you like snapdragons?
....

Do you like azaleas?   ....?
....

1. couch/sofa 長沙發
2. cushion 墊子
3. (throw) pillow 靠枕
4. club chair 扶手椅
5. love seat 鴛鴦椅
6. coffee table 咖啡桌
7. end table 茶几
8. lamp 燈
9. lamp shade 燈罩
10. wall unit 靠牆組合櫃
11. bookcase 書櫥

12. book 書
13. window 窗
14. drape 窗簾
15. plant 植物
16. planter 花盆
17. flowers 花
18. vase 花瓶
19. fireplace 壁爐
20. (fireplace) screen 遮火板
21. mantel 壁爐架
22. picture 畫像

23. (picture) frame 相架
24. side table 邊桌／小茶几
25. ottoman 軟墊長椅
26. rug 地毯
27. floor 地板
28. ceiling 天花板

> The vase is <u>in front of</u> the window.
> The wall unit is <u>behind</u> the couch.
> The book is <u>on</u> the side table.

The planter is .... the drapes.
The lamp is .... the end table.
The side table is ....the ottoman.

The fireplace screen is .... the fireplace.
The coffee table is .... the rug.

THE DINING ROOM 飯廳

1. centerpiece
   餐桌中央花飾
2. wine glass 酒杯
3. water glass 水杯
4. napkin ring 餐巾套環
5. napkin 餐巾
6. plate 盤子/碟子
7. (dining room) table 餐桌
8. chair 椅
9. armchair 靠手椅
10. (salad) fork 吃沙拉
    用短叉
11. (dinner) fork 餐叉
12. knife 餐刀
13. soupspoon 湯匙
14. teaspoon 茶匙
15. (serving) bowl 上菜碗
16. server 上菜用的器具
17. cup 茶杯
18. saucer 茶碟
19. teapot 茶壺
20. sideboard/buffet 餐具櫥
21. mirror 鏡
22. chandelier 枝形吊燈

Where is the salad fork?
It's <u>to the left of</u> the dinner fork.

Where is the teaspoon?
It's <u>to the right of</u> the soupspoon.

Where is the soupspoon?
It's .... the teaspoon.

Where is the dinner fork?
It's .... the salad fork.

Where is the knife?
It's .... the soupspoon.

THE BEDROOM 睡房／臥室

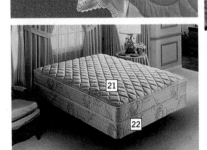

1. night table/nightstand 牀頭櫃
2. headboard 牀頭板
3. throw pillow 靠枕
4. bed 牀
5. bedspread 牀罩
6. dust ruffle 縐邊牀裙／牀幕
7. carpet 地毯
8. lamp 燈
9. chest (of drawers) 五斗櫃
10. drawer 抽屜
11. handle/pull 手柄

12. mirror 鏡
13. dresser 梳妝枱
14. pillowcase 枕頭套
15. pillow 枕頭
16. (fitted) sheet 套褥牀單
17. (flat) sheet 褥單
18. comforter/quilt 被子
19. electric blanket 電毯
20. (heat) control （熱）調節器
21. mattress 牀褥
22. box spring 彈簧牀座

The throw pillow is <u>on top of</u> the bedspread.
The box spring is <u>underneath</u> the mattress.

The comforter is .... the flat sheet.
The fitted sheet is .... the flat sheet.
The carpet is .... the bed.
The mattress is .... the box spring.

THE BATHROOM 浴室

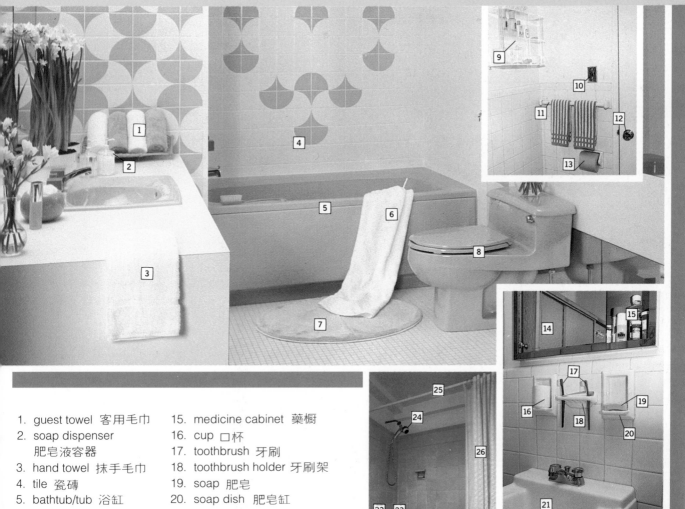

1. guest towel 客用毛巾
2. soap dispenser 肥皂液容器
3. hand towel 抹手毛巾
4. tile 瓷磚
5. bathtub/tub 浴缸
6. bath towel 浴巾
7. bath mat/bath rug 揩腳墊
8. toilet 廁桶
9. shelf 擱架
10. light switch 電燈開關
11. towel rack 毛巾架
12. doorknob 門把手
13. toilet paper 廁紙
14. mirror 鏡

15. medicine cabinet 藥櫥
16. cup 口杯
17. toothbrush 牙刷
18. toothbrush holder 牙刷架
19. soap 肥皂
20. soap dish 肥皂缸
21. sink 水池 / 水槽
22. hot water faucet 熱水龍頭
23. cold water faucet 冷水龍頭
24. shower head 淋浴噴頭 / 蓮蓬頭
25. shower curtain rod 淋浴簾支條
26. shower curtain 淋浴簾
27. washcloth 毛巾

Where's the medicine cabinet?
It's <u>above</u> the sink.

Where's the sink?
It's <u>below</u> the medicine cabinet.

Where's the light switch?
It's .... the towel rack.

Where's the toilet paper?
It's .... the towel rack.

Where's the soap dish?
It's .... the medicine cabinet.

Where's the cup?
It's .... the sink.

1. oven 烤爐
2. spice rack 調味品架
3. spices 調味品
4. canister 小罐
5. trivet 三腳架
6. sink 洗滌槽
7. faucet 水龍頭
8. cake stand 蛋糕架
9. cookbook 食譜
10. freezer 冰凍箱
11. refrigerator
    電冰箱／雪櫃
12. dishwasher 洗碟機

13. stove/range 火爐
14. burner 爐灶
15. (copper) pot 銅鍋
16. coffee pot 咖啡壺
17. creamer 奶油缸
18. cup 杯
19. saucer 碟
20. counter 櫃枱
21. bowl 碗
22. plate 碟
23. drawer 抽屜
24. cupboard/cabinet 碗櫃
25. (door) handle（門）把手

26. cutting board 案板
27. (paring) knife 削皮刀
28. dish towel 擦碗布／抹布
29. Saran wrap/
    plastic wrap 保鮮紙
30. aluminum foil 鋁箔
31. pot holder 隔熱手套

Where's the canister?
It's <u>on</u> the counter.

Where's the bowl?
It's <u>next to</u> the plate.

Where's the cup?
It's .... the saucer.

Where's the dishwasher?
It's .... the freezer.

Where's the pot?
It's .... the stove.

KITCHENWARE 廚房用具

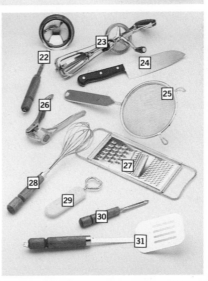

1. double boiler 雙層蒸鍋
2. lid/cover 鍋蓋
3. pot 烹飪鍋
4. casserole 燉鍋
5. frying pan/skillet
   煎鍋／平底鍋
6. handle 鍋柄
7. roaster 烤鍋
8. cake pan 煎餅鍋
9. bowl 碗
10. cookie sheet
    烤／餅乾鐵盤
11. rolling pin 趕麵杖
12. measuring cup 量杯
13. measuring spoon 量匙
14. coffee maker 咖啡壺
15. microwave oven 微波爐
16. can opener 開罐器
17. blender 攪拌器
18. food processor
    食品加工器
19. toaster oven
    焗爐／烤箱
20. (electric) mixer
    （電）攪拌器
21. toaster 烤麵包器
22. ladle 長柄杓子
23. (hand) beater/egg
    beater 打蛋器
24. knife 刀
25. strainer 篩子
26. garlic press 碎蒜器
27. grater 擦板
28. whisk 打蛋器
29. bottle opener 開瓶器
30. peeler 削皮刀
31. spatula 鍋鏟

What's a <u>toaster</u> for?	For making toast.

| What's a .... for? | For making cookies. | ....? | For making roasts. |
| What's a .... for ? | For making coffee. | ....? | For opening cans. |

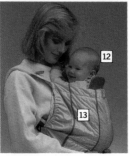

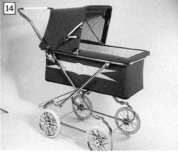

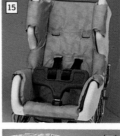

1. changing pad 可換墊
2. child 小孩
3. bar 圍欄
4. crib 兒童床
5. chest (of drawers) 五斗櫃
6. lamp 燈
7. teddy bear 玩具熊
8. stuffed animal 玩具動物
9. baby chair 兒童椅
10. rug 地毯
11. stroller 嬰兒手推車
12. baby/infant 嬰兒
13. baby carrier 嬰兒背帶
14. carriage 嬰兒車
15. car seat 車座
16. highchair 嬰兒高椅
17. playpen 嬰兒圈欄
18. baby seat 嬰兒座位
19. bib 小孩圍嘴
20. nipple 奶嘴
21. (baby) bottle 奶瓶
22. cap/top 奶瓶蓋
23. food warmer 食物保暖器
24. (baby) clothes 嬰兒服裝
25. diaper 尿布

Put the baby in the <u>playpen</u>.
19 Put the <u>bib</u> on the baby.

11 Put the baby in the ....
25 Put the .... on the baby.

16 Put the baby in the ....
24 Put the .... on the baby.

THE PLAYGROUND 遊樂場

1. see-saw/teeter-totter 蹺蹺板
2. slide 滑梯
3. toddler/child 學步的小孩
4. tricycle 三輪車
5. swing 鞦韆
6. bench 條凳
7. jungle gym 攀爬架
8. sandbox 沙箱
9. sand 沙
10. pail 小桶
11. shovel 小鏟
12. overalls 工裝褲
13. sneakers 膠鞋
14. water fountain 噴水池
15. doll 玩偶
16. doll carriage 玩具車
17. skateboard 滑板
18. kite 風箏

| Where is he? | 4 He's <u>on the tricycle</u>. |
| Where is she? | 6 She's <u>on the bench</u>. |

Where is he?   7 He's ....
Where is she?   1 She's ....
..........?   2 ....
..........?   17 ....

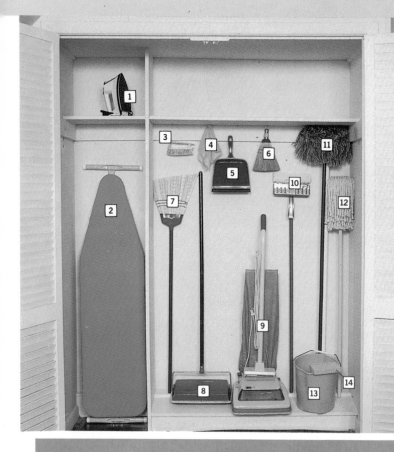

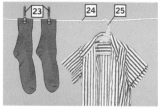

1. iron 熨斗
2. ironing board 熨衣板
3. scrub brush 擦洗毛刷
4. dust cloth 抹布
5. dustpan 簸箕
6. whisk broom 小掃帚／小掃把
7. broom 掃帚／掃把
8. carpet sweeper 地毯清掃器
9. vacuum cleaner 真空吸塵器
10. (sponge) mop 海綿拖把

11. (dust) mop （撢塵）拖把
12. (wet) mop 濕水拖把
13. bucket/pail 水桶
14. sponge 海綿
15. washer/washing machine 洗衣機
16. dryer 乾衣機／烘乾機
17. detergent 清潔劑
18. measuring cup 量杯
19. laundry 要洗或已洗的衣服

20. hamper 有蓋提籃
21. laundry bag 髒衣服袋
22. laundry basket 髒衣服簍
23. clothespin 晒衣夾
24. clothesline 晒衣繩
25. hanger 衣架
26. three-pronged plug 三腳插頭
27. (wall) socket/outlet 插座
28. bulb 燈泡
29. extension cord 拖線

The carpet sweeper is <u>to the right of</u> the broom.
The broom is <u>to the left of</u> the carpet sweeper.

The broom is .... the ironing board.
The vacuum cleaner is .... the sponge mop.
The wet mop is .... the dust mop.

The dust pan is .... the whisk broom.
The .... is to the left of the ....
The .... is to the right of the ....

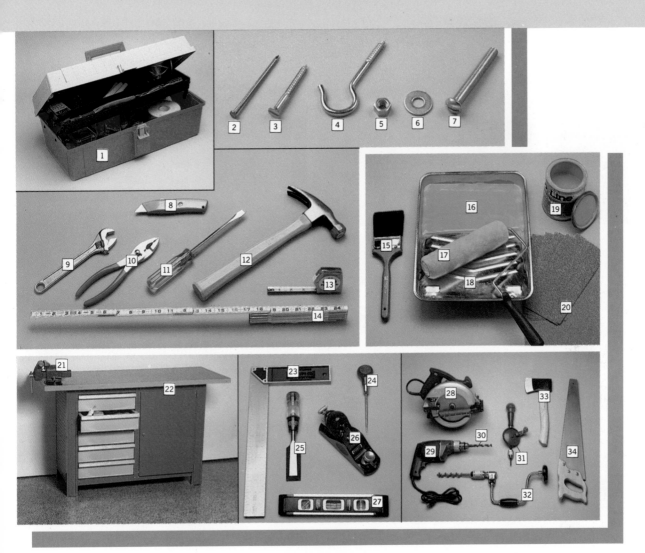

1. toolbox 工具箱
2. nail 釘
3. screw 螺絲釘
4. hook 掛鈎
5. nut 螺帽
6. washer 墊圈
7. bolt 螺栓
8. utility knife 萬能刀
9. wrench 板手
10. pliers 鉗
11. screwdriver 起子／螺絲錐

12. hammer 鎚
13. tape measure 卷尺
14. folding rule 折尺
15. paintbrush/brush 漆刷／刷子
16. paint 油漆
17. (paint) roller 油漆滾筒
18. pan 盤
19. (paint) can 油漆罐
20. sandpaper 砂紙
21. vise 老虎鉗
22. workbench 工作台

23. square 直角尺
24. awl 錐子
25. chisel 鑿子
26. plane 鉋刀
27. level 水平儀
28. power saw 電鋸
29. electric drill 電鑽
30. bit 鑽頭
31. hand drill 手鑽
32. brace 手搖曲柄鑽
33. hatchet 短柄小斧
34. saw 手鋸

| Have you ever used a <u>hammer</u>? | Yes, I have./No, I haven't. |
| Have you ever used an <u>awl</u>? | Yes, I have./No, I haven't. |

Have you ever used a ....?   ....?   ....
Have you ever used a ....?   ....

1. video cassette recorder/VCR 錄（放）影機
2. (video) cassette 錄影帶
3. remote control 遙控
4. television/TV 電視機
5. screen 螢光幕
6. stereo system 立體聲系統
7. record 唱片
8. turntable 唱盤
9. amplifier 放大器
10. tuner 調諧器
11. tape deck/cassette deck 錄音機

12. speaker 揚聲器
13. compact disc player 鐳射唱機
14. compact disc/CD 鐳射唱片
15. radio 收音機
16. clock radio 定時開關收音機
17. tape recorder/cassette player 卡式錄音機
18. personal cassette player/Walkman 耳筒錄音機／隨身聽（台灣）
19. headphone 耳筒
20. (audio) cassette/tape 錄音帶
21. answering machine 答話機／答錄機
22. telephone 電話

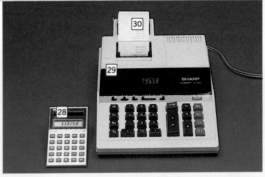

23. computer 電腦	34. plug converter 換路插頭
24. display screen/monitor 顯示屏	35. electronic typewriter 電子打字機
25. floppy disc/diskette 軟性磁碟片	36. electric typewriter 電動打字機
26. keyboard 鍵盤	37. disc camera 碟式照像機
27. printer 打印機	38. disc film 碟式底片
28. pocket calculator 袖珍計算機	39. camera 照像機
29. calculator 計算機	40. lens 鏡頭
30. tape 紙帶	41. flash 閃光燈
31. adapter 調適器	42. film 菲林／底片
32. battery 電池	43. video camera 電視攝影機
33. voltage converter 變壓器	44. slide projector 幻燈機

Would you like to have an <u>answering machine</u>?
Yes, I would./No, I wouldn't. I'd rather have a <u>tape recorder</u>.

Would you like to have a ....?   Would you like to have a ....?   ....?
....

CONSTRUCTION 建築

1. construction worker
   建築工人
2. hook 吊鈎
3. girder 樑
4. ladder 梯
5. hard hat 安全帽
6. tool belt 工具腰帶
7. scaffold 手腳架／鷹架
8. crane 起重機
9. excavation site 挖掘區
10. dump truck 傾卸車
11. frontend loader
    前卸式裝載機
12. backhoe 挖土機／怪手

13. blasting mat 爆破保護墊
14. cement mixer 水泥拌和機
15. cement 水泥
16. trowel 泥刀
17. brick 磚
18. level 水平儀
19. wheelbarrow 手推車
20. jack hammer/
    pneumatic drill 風鑽
21. shovel 鏟
22. sledge hammer 大錘
23. pickax 鎬

8 Have you ever seen a crane?
   Yes, I have./No, I haven't.

12 Have you ever seen a ....?
....

9 Have you ever seen an .... ?
....

10 ....?
....

1. mountain 山
2. peak 峯
3. meadow 草原
4. valley 谷
5. hill 小山
6. tree 樹
7. grass 草
8. field 田野
9. cliff 峭壁／懸崖
10. rock 岩／礁
11. forest 森林
12. lake 湖
13. pond 池塘
14. river 河
15. stream/brook 溪
16. waterfall 瀑布
17. desert 沙漠
18. dune 沙丘

⏐1⏐ Are there any <u>mountains</u> near here?
   Yes, there are./No, there aren't.

⏐5⏐ Are there any .... near here?
   ....

⏐12⏐ Are there any .... near here?
   ....

⏐14⏐ ....?
   ....

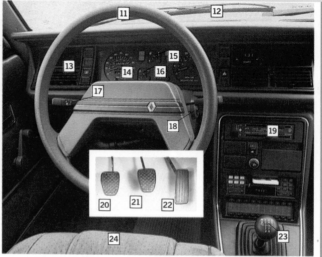

1. gas station　加油站
2. gas pump　油泵
3. nozzle　噴嘴
4. hose　軟管
5. attendant　服務員
6. (rear) windshield（後）擋風玻璃
7. trunk　行李箱
8. license plate　車牌
9. taillight　尾燈
10. bumper　保險槓
11. steering wheel　駕駛盤
12. windshield wiper 雨刷／水撥
13. dashboard/
　　instrument panel　儀錶板

14. speedometer　速度表
15. fuel gauge　油量表
16. temperature gauge　溫度計
17. turn signal　轉向示警燈／
　　方向燈
18. ignition　點火
19. heater　加熱器
20. clutch　離合器
21. brake　制動器／刹車
22. gas pedal/
　　accelerator　油門踏板
23. gearshift　變速桿
24. seat　座位
25. heater hose　加熱器軟管

26. air filter　空氣過濾器
27. battery　電池
28. engine　發動機
29. alternator　交流發電機
30. cool air duct　冷空氣管
31. coolant recovery tank 冷却劑回收箱／桶
32. radiator　散熱器
33. sedan　轎車
34. hubcap　轂蓋
35. tire　輪胎
36. convertible　敞篷車
37. station wagon　客貨兩用車
38. pick-up truck　小噸位貨車

What's that called – a <u>hubcap</u> or a <u>tire</u>?　35 It's a <u>tire</u>.

What's that called – a clutch or a brake?　　　　　　　　　21 It's a ....
What's that called – a fuel gauge or a temperature gauge?　15 It's a ....
What's that called – a convertible or a sedan?　　　　　　33 ....
What's that called – a battery or a radiator?　　　　　　　27 ....

A. The Train Station 火車站

1. information booth　詢問處
2. clock　鐘
3. ticket counter　售票處
4. arrival and departure board
   列車到站及離站顯示牌
5. train　火車
6. track　軌道
7. platform　月台
8. passenger car　客車
9. porter/redcap　搬運工人
10. passenger　乘客

B. The Bus Station 巴士站

11. bus　巴士

12. driver　司機
13. suitcase　衣箱／行李箱
14. luggage compartment
    行李格（箱）

C. The Taxi Stand
計程車停車場

15. taxi　計程車／的士（香港）
16. radio call sign　無線電招喚牌
17. off-duty sign　不營業牌
18. (door) handle　（門）把手
19. door　車門

D. Schedule
行車時間表

PELHAM TO NEW YORK

MONDAY TO FRIDAY, EXCEPT HOLIDAYS

Leave	Arrive	Leave	Arrive	Leave	Arrive
Pelham	New York	Pelham	New York	Pelham	New York
AM	AM	AM	AM	PM	PM
5:32	6:00	F10:40	F11:10	FT 5:33	F 6:03
6:02	6:30	11:03	11:33	F 6:03	6:33
6:32	7:00	11:33	12:03	F 6:33	F 7:03
6:52	7:20	12:03	12:33	F 7:03	7:33
7:12	7:40	F12:33	F 1:03	F 7:33	F 8:03
7:28	X 8:00	1:03	1:33	Y 8:03	8:33
F 7:44	F 8:14	1:33	2:03	F 8:33	F 9:03
7:59	8:28	2:03	2:33	9:03	9:33
8:17	8:46	F 2:33	F 3:03	9:33	10:03
F 8:32	F 9:01	3:03	3:33	F10:33	F11:03
F 9:05	F 9:35	F 3:33	F 4:03	11:33	12:03
F 9:22	F 9:52	4:03	4:33	12:58	1:28
9:43	10:12	F 4:33	F 5:03	——	——
F10:03	F10:33	Y 5:03	5:33		
AM	AM	PM	PM		

SATURDAY, SUNDAY & HOLIDAYS

Leave	Arrive	Leave	Arrive	Leave	Arrive
AM	AM	PM	PM	PM	PM
7:03	7:33	12:33	1:03	7:03	7:33
8:03	8:33	F 1:03	F 2:03	F 7:33	F 8:03
F 8:33	F 9:03	2:33	3:03	8:33	9:03
9:03	9:33	F 3:33	F 4:03	F 9:33	F10:03
F 9:33	F10:03	4:33	5:03	10:33	11:03
F10:33	F11:03	S 5:03	S 5:33	11:33	12:03
F11:33	F12:03	F 5:33	F 6:03	12:58	1:28
AM	AM	PM	PM	PM	PM

Where should we meet?　A At the station.
Where should we meet?　5 On the train.

Where should we meet?　B At the ....?　7 On the ....
Where should we meet?　11 On the ....?　1 At the ....

A. Highway 公路

1. overpass 上跨橋／天橋
2. underpass 橋下通道／地下道
3. broken line 虛線
4. solid line 實線
5. shoulder 路肩
6. divider 分隔線
7. left lane 左車道
8. middle lane 中間車道
9. right lane 右車道
10. van 有蓋小型貨車
11. car 汽車
12. bus 巴士
13. truck 卡車

B. Tollgate
車輛通行收費關口

14. tollbooth 收費亭
15. exact change lane 不找零（錢）車道
16. change lane 找零錢車道

C. Tunnel 隧道

17. street light 路燈

D. Bridge 橋

E. Road 公路
18. dirt road 砂土路
19. curve sign 彎道牌
20. double yellow lines 雙黃線

F. Intersection 十字路口
21. crosswalk 行人穿越道／行人橫道
22. street 街
23. corner 拐角

G. Railroad Crossing
鐵路交叉點
24. traffic light 交通燈
25. railroad track 鐵路軌道

H. Road Signs
公路標誌
26. route sign 公路編號標誌
27. stop sign 停車標誌
28. yield sign 讓路標誌
29. do not enter sign 不准駛入標誌
30. school crossing sign
學校區人行道標誌
31. speed limit sign 限速標誌
32. no U-turn sign 禁止後轉標誌
33. no left turn sign 禁止左轉
34. no right turn sign 禁止右轉
35. no trucks sign
貨車不准駛入標誌
36. hill sign 斜坡標誌
37. slippery when wet sign
路面濕滑標誌
38. telephone sign 電話標誌
39. bike route sign 自行車道標誌

Is that a <u>stop sign</u>? 27 Yes, it is.
Is that a <u>route sign</u>? 31 No, it isn't. It's a <u>speed limit sign</u>.

Is that a yield sign? 28 .... Is that a telephone sign? 38 ....
Is that a bike route sign? 30 .... Is that a hill sign? 37 ....

THE AIRPORT 飛機場

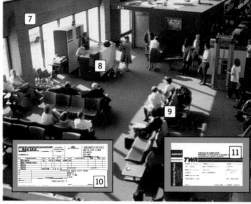

A. The Terminal
機場大樓

1. ticket agent 售票員
2. ticket counter 售票處
3. suitcase 小提箱
4. arrival and departure board
   飛機到達及起飛顯示牌
5. security check 安全檢查
6. security guard 警衛員
7. gate 閘／門
8. check-in counter 登記櫃枱
9. waiting room 候機室
10. ticket 機票
11. boarding pass 登機証
12. baggage claim area
    行李領取處
13. porter/skycap 搬運工人
14. luggage carrier 行李車
15. luggage 行李
16. (luggage) carousel
    行李旋轉輸送機
17. (baggage) claim check
    行李領取單
18. customs 海關
19. customs officer 海關官員
20. documents 文件
21. passport 護照

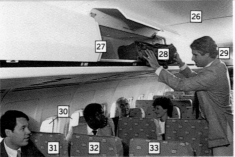

B. On Board 在機內

22. cockpit 飛機駕駛艙
23. pilot/captain 駕駛員／機長
24. co-pilot 副駕駛員
25. instrument panel 儀錶板
26. cabin 機艙
27. overhead (luggage) compartment 機艙頂板行李櫃
28. carry-on luggage/ carry-on bag 隨身行李

29. passenger 乘客
30. window 窗
31. window seat 靠窗座位
32. middle seat 中間座位
33. aisle seat 靠通道座位
34. flight attendant 空中服務員
35. tray table 托盤桌
36. tray 托盤
37. armrest 靠手

C. The Runway 跑道

38. terminal 機場大樓

39. jet (plane) 噴氣式飛機
40. tail 機尾
41. jet engine 噴氣式發動機
42. wing 機翼
43. runway 跑道
44. control tower 指揮塔／塔台
45. rotor 旋翼
46. helicopter 直昇機
47. hangar 機庫

Where's the ticket agent?	He's at the ticket counter.
Where's the pilot?	He's in the cockpit.
Where's the tray?	It's on the tray table.

Where's the security guard? He's at the ....
Where's the check-in counter? It's at the ....
Where's the passenger? He's in the ....

Where's the carry-on bag? It's in the ....
Where's the luggage? It's on the ....
Where's the plane? It's on the ....

THE WATERFRONT 濱水區

61

1. harbor　海港
2. pier/dock　碼頭
3. passenger ship/ocean liner
　　客輪／遠洋郵輪
4. port　左舷
5. starboard　右舷
6. bow　船頭
7. stern　船尾
8. cargo ship/freighter　貨輪
9. cargo　貨物
10. deck　甲板
11. winch　絞車
12. line　纜
13. derrick　搖臂吊機
14. dock worker/longshoreman
　　碼頭裝卸工人
15. crane　起重機
16. (oil) tanker　油輪
17. buoy　浮標
18. barge　駁船
19. tugboat　拖船
20. ferry　渡船／渡輪

3 Have you ever been on a <u>passenger ship</u>?
　Yes, I have./No, I haven't.

19 Have you ever been on a ....?
....

20 Have you ever been on a ....?
....

8 ....?
....

THE BEACH 沙灘

1. hotel　酒店／飯店
2. boardwalk　木板路
3. sand　沙
4. (beach) blanket　（沙灘）氈子
5. (beach) towel　（沙灘）大毛巾
6. trash can　垃圾桶
7. (beach) chair　（沙灘）椅
8. (beach) umbrella　（沙灘）太陽傘
9. lounge chair　躺椅
10. lifeguard stand　救生員瞭望台
11. lifeguard　救生員
12. wave　波浪
13. ocean　海洋
14. (beach) ball　（沙灘）球
15. (beach) hat/sun hat　（沙灘）遮陽帽
16. sand castle　沙堡
17. bathing suit　游泳衣
18. pail/bucket　桶
19. seashell　貝殼
20. rock　岩石

| Do you usually take a <u>hat</u> to the beach? | Yes, I do./No, I don't. |
| Do you usually take an <u>umberella</u> to the beach? | Yes, I do./No, I don/t. |

Do you usually take a .... to the beach?　　　　　　..........
Do you usually take a .... to the beach?　　　　　　..........
..........?　　　　　　..........

WATER SPORTS 水上運動

A. Swimming 游泳
1. swimmer 游泳者
2. swimming pool 游泳池

B. Diving 跳水
3. diver 跳水者
4. diving board 跳板

C. Snorkeling 潛游
5. snorkeler 潛游者
6. snorkel 潛游通氣管

D. Scuba Diving 深水潛水
7. scuba diver 深水潛水者
8. wet suit 潛泳衣

9. (air) tank 氣瓶
10. mask 面罩

E. Fishing 釣魚
11. fisherman 釣魚人
12. fishing rod 釣桿
13. (fishing) line 釣絲

F. Surfing 滑浪
14. surfer 滑浪者
15. surf 浪花
16. surfboard 滑浪板

G. Windsurfing 滑浪風帆
17. windsurfer 駕風帆者
18. sail 帆

H. Sailing 駕帆船
19. sailboat 帆船
20. mast 桅桿

I. Waterskiing 滑水
21. water-skier 滑水者
22. water ski 滑水橇
23. towrope 拖纜
24. motorboat 汽船

J. Rowing 划船
25. rower 划船者
26. rowboat 划船
27. oar 划槳

K. Canoeing 划獨木舟
28. canoeist 划獨木舟
29. canoe 獨木舟
30. paddle 小槳

L. Kayaking 划皮艇
31. kayaker 划皮艇的人
32. kayak 皮艇

M. White Water Rafting 划橡皮艇過激流
33. raft 橡皮艇
34. life jacket 救生衣
35. rapids 急流

Does a canoeist use a <u>paddle</u>?	30	Yes, he does.
Does a rower use a <u>paddle</u>?	27	No, he doesn't. He uses an <u>oar</u>.

Does a surfer use a surfboard? 16 ....
Does a fisherman use a mask? 12 ....

Does a scuba diver use a life jacket? 8 ....
Does a water-skier use a towrope? 23 ....

WINTER SPORTS 冬季運動

A. Sledding 滑雪橇
1. sled 雪橇／雪車

B. Downhill Skiing 滑雪下山
2. skier 滑冰者
3. pole 雪杖
4. (ski) boot 滑雪鞋
5. ski 雪板
6. chair lift 上山吊椅

C. Cross Country Skiing 越野滑雪
7. skier 滑雪者
8. ski cap 滑雪帽
9. trail 滑道

D. Figure Skating 花式溜冰
10. figure skater 花式溜冰者
11. figure skate 溜冰鞋
12. blade 冰刀

E. Ice Skating 刀式溜冰
13. skater 溜冰者
14. skate 溜冰鞋
15. ice 冰

F. Bobsledding 滑大雪橇
16. bobsled 大雪橇
17. helmet 頭盔

G. Snowmobiling 開機動雪車
18. snowmobile 機動雪車

Do you prefer <u>downhill skiing</u> or <u>cross country skiing</u>?
I prefer <u>downhill skiing</u>.

Do you prefer sledding or snowmobiling?   Do you prefer .... or ....?   ....?
I prefer ....   I prefer ....

15. home (plate) 本壘板
16. umpire 裁判員
17. spectator 觀眾
18. baseball 棒球
19. batter 擊球員
20. bat 球棒
21. helmet 防護帽
22. uniform 球衣
23. catcher 接手
24. mask 面罩
25. (baseball) glove/mitt 捧球手套
26. shin guard 護脛

B. Football 美式足
27. (football) field 足球場
28. fullback/ runningback 後衛
29. halfback/ runningback 中衛
30. right end/ wide receiver 右翼
31. tight end 右翼鋒
32. right tackle 右擒拿手
33. right guard 右衛
34. center 中鋒
35. quarterback 四分衛
36. left guard 左衛
37. left tackle 左擒拿手
38. left end/ wide receiver 左翼
39. football 橄欖球

A. Baseball 棒球
1. stadium 運動場
2. stadium lights 運動場照明
3. foul line 邊線
4. (pitcher's) mound 投手區
5. pitcher 投手
6. first base 一壘
7. first baseman 一壘手
8. outfielder 外野手
9. second baseman 二壘手
10. second base 二壘
11. shortstop 游擊手
12. third baseman 三壘手
13. coach 教練
14. third base 三壘

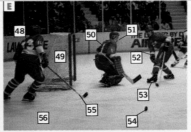

49. goal　球門
50. goalie　守門員
51. mask　面罩
52. glove　手套
53. skate　冰鞋
54. puck　冰球
55. (hockey) stick　冰球桿
56. ice　冰場地

F. Tennis　網球

57. (tennis) player
　　網球運動員
58. (tennis) racket　網球拍
59. (tennis) ball　網球
60. net　網球網
61. (tennis) court　網球場
62. baseline　底線

G. Wrestling　摔跤

63. wrestler　摔跤者
64. mat　摔跤墊

H. Karate　空手道

65. (black) belt　黑腰帶

I. Boxing　拳擊

66. boxer　拳擊者
67. (boxing) glove　拳擊手套
68. trunks　運動短褲
69. referee　裁判
70. rope　圍繩
71. ring　拳擊台

J. Horse Racing　賽馬

72. gate　閘

C. Basketball　籃球

40. (basketball) player
　　籃球運動員
41. basketball　籃球
42. backboard　籃板
43. basket　球籃

D. Soccer　英式足球

44. (soccer) player
　　足球運動員
45. goal　球門
46. (soccer) ball　足球
47. (soccer) field　足球場

E. Ice Hockey　冰球

48. (hockey) player
　　冰球員

B　Do they play <u>football</u> in your country?
　Yes, they do./No, they don't. They play <u>soccer</u>.

C　Do they play .... in your country?
....

A　Do they play .... in your country?
....

E　..........?
....

A. Jogging 慢跑
1. jogger 慢跑者

B. Running 賽跑
2. runner 賽跑者

C. Cycling 騎腳踏車
3. cyclist 騎腳踏車者
4. helmet 頭盔
5. bicycle/bike 腳踏車
6. (bicycle) pack （腳踏車）掛包
7. wheel 輪

D. Horseback Riding 騎馬
8. (horseback) rider 騎馬者
9. horse 馬
10. reins 馬韁繩
11. saddle 馬鞍
12. stirrup 鐙

E. Archery 射箭
13. archer 射箭者
14. bow 弓
15. arrow 箭
16. target 靶

F. Golf 打高爾夫球
17. golfer 打高爾夫球者
18. (golf) club 球桿
19. (golf) ball 高爾夫球
20. hole 球洞
21. green 果嶺

G. Hiking 徒步旅行
22. hiker 徒步旅行者
23. backpack 背囊
24. hiking boot 步行靴
25. trail 小徑

H. Camping 露營
26. camper 露營者
27. tent 帳篷

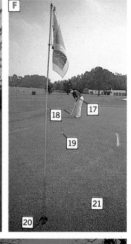

I. Volleyball 排球
28. (volleyball) player 排球運動員
29. volleyball 排球
30. net 球網

J. Rollerskating 輪式溜冰
31. roller skater 輪式溜冰者
32. roller skate 輪式溜冰鞋
33. rink 溜冰場

K. Bowling 保齡球
34. bowler 打保齡球者
35. (bowling) ball 保齡球
36. gutter 球坑
37. alley 保齡球場
38. pin 球瓶

L. Ping Pong/ Table Tennis 乒乓球
39. (ping pong) player 乒乓球運動員
40. paddle 球拍
41. (ping pong) ball 乒乓球
42. net 乒乓球網
43. (ping pong) table 乒乓球台

M. Handball 手球
44. (handball) player 打手球者
45. glove 手套

N. Squash 壁球
46. (squash) player 打壁球者
47. (squash) racket 壁球拍
48. (squash) ball 壁球

O. Badminton 羽毛球
49. (badminton) player 打羽毛球的人
50. (badminton) racket 羽毛球拍
51. shuttlecock 羽毛球
52. court 球場

Do you like jogging?
Yes, I do./No, I don't. I prefer cycling.

Do you like ....?
....
Do you like ....?
....
..........?
....

ENTERTAINMENT 娛樂

69

A. Symphony 交響樂
1. orchestra 管弦樂隊
2. podium 指揮臺
3. conductor 樂隊指揮者
4. (sheet) music 樂譜
5. music stand 樂譜架

B. Opera 歌劇
6. chorus 合唱隊
7. singer 歌手

C. Ballet 芭蕾舞
8. ballerina 芭蕾舞女演員
9. ballet dancer 芭蕾舞男演員
10. toe shoe 芭蕾舞鞋

D. Theater 劇場
11. actress 女演員
12. actor 男演員
13. stage 舞台
14. audience 觀眾
15. aisle 通道
16. spotlight 聚光燈
17. footlights 腳燈
18. orchestra pit 樂隊池

E. Movie Theater 電影院
19. marquee （戲院外）遮簷
20. billboard 廣告招貼板

F. Rock Concert 搖滾舞音樂會
21. singer/vocalist 歌手

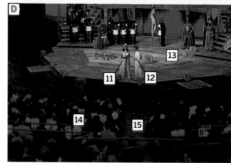
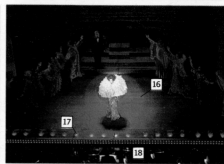

Have you ever been to a <u>ballet</u>?
Yes, I have./No, I haven't.

Have you ever been to a ....?   ....?
....

Have you ever been to an ....?   ....?
....

MUSICAL INSTRUMENTS 樂器

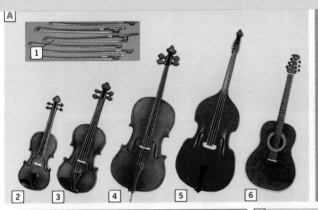

A. Strings 弦樂器
1. bow 琴弓
2. violin 小提琴
3. viola 中提琴
4. cello 大提琴
5. bass 低音提琴
6. guitar 吉他／大弦琴

B. Brass 銅管樂器
7. trombone 長號／伸縮喇叭
8. French horn 法國號
9. tuba 大號／低音大喇叭
10. trumpet 小號／小喇叭

C. Woodwinds 木管樂器
11. flute 長笛
12. recorder 直笛
13. oboe 雙簧管
14. clarinet 單簧管
15. saxophone 薩克管
16. bassoon 巴松管

D. Percussion 敲擊樂器
17. cymbal 鈸
18. drum 鼓
19. xylophone 木琴

E. Other Instruments 其他樂器
20. piano 鋼琴
21. accordion 手風琴
22. harmonica 口琴

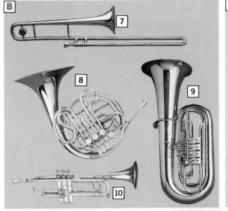

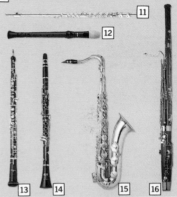

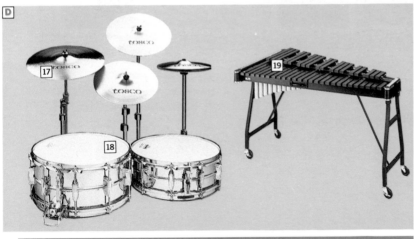

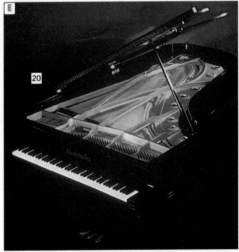

The cello is <u>larger than</u> the violin.
The recorder is <u>smaller than</u> the flute.

The French horn is .... the trumpet.
The harmonica is .... the accordion.
The violin is .... the cello.
The bass is .... the viola.

A. The Zoo 動物園

1. lion 獅
2. mane 鬃
3. tiger 虎
4. paw 爪
5. tail 尾
6. leopard 豹
7. spot 豹斑

8. elephant 象
9. tusk 象牙
10. trunk 象鼻
11. rhinoceros 犀牛
12. horn 角
13. hippopotamus 河馬
14. bear 熊
15. polar bear 北極熊

16. buffalo 水牛
17. zebra 斑馬
18. stripe 斑紋
19. camel 駱駝
20. hump 駝峰
21. giraffe 長頸鹿
22. deer 鹿
23. antler 鹿角

24. llama 駱馬
25. koala bear 無尾熊
26. kangaroo 袋鼠
27. pouch 肚袋
28. monkey 猴
29. gorilla 大猩猩
30. fox 狐狸
31. raccoon 浣熊

Do zebras has <u>stripes</u>?	18	Yes, they do.
Do leopards have <u>stripes</u>?	7	No, they don't. They have <u>spots</u>.

Do lions have manes?   2..........   Do camels have humps?   20..........

Do elephants have manes?   10..........   ....?   ....

Do rhinoceroses have antlers?   12..........

32. alligator 美洲鱷
33. snake 蛇
34. tortoise 龜
35. lizard 蜥蜴
36. frog 蛙
37. turtle 鱉／甲魚

B. Pets 寵物
38. puppy 小狗
39. dog 狗
40. paw 狗爪
41. kitten 小貓

42. cat 貓
43. whiskers 鬚
44. parrot 鸚鵡
45. parakeet 長尾小鸚鵡
46. gerbil 沙鼠
47. tail 尾
48. hamster 倉鼠
49. guinea pig 天竺鼠
50. rabbit 兔
51. goldfish 金魚
52. (fish) bowl 魚缸
53. tropical fish 熱帶魚

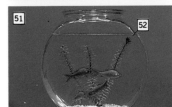

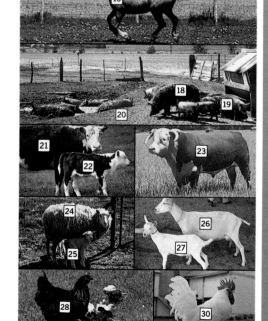

1. farmland 農田
2. farmhouse 農舍
3. barn 穀倉
4. silo 青貯塔
5. barnyard（穀倉旁）場地
6. fence 籬笆
7. pond 池塘
8. wheat field 麥田
9. combine 聯合收割機
10. vegetable field 菜田
11. farmer 農夫
12. tractor 牽引機／拖拉機
13. furrow 犁溝
14. crop 農作物
15. irrigation system 灌溉系統
16. horse 馬
17. mane 鬃
18. pig 豬
19. piglet 小豬
20. pigpen/pig sty 豬欄
21. cow 母牛
22. calf 小牛
23. bull 公牛
24. sheep 綿羊
25. lamb 小羊
26. goat 山羊
27. kid 小山羊
28. chicken/hen 小雞／母雞
29. chick 小雞
30. rooster 公雞

A calf is <u>younger than</u> a cow.
A goat is <u>older than</u> a kid.

A chick is .... a hen.
A goat is .... a kid.
A pig is ....
A lamb is ....
A cow is ....

FISH & SEA ANIMALS
魚及海洋動物

A. Fish 魚類

1. shark 鯊
2. snout 鼻子
3. fin 鰭
4. tail 尾
5. bass 鱸魚
6. scale 鱗
7. trout 鱒魚
8. gill 鰓
9. angelfish 神仙魚
10. sunfish 翻車魚
11. eel 鰻／鱔

B. Sea Animals 海洋動物

12. octopus 鱆魚
13. tentacle 觸鬚
14. whale 鯨
15. dolphin 海豚
16. seal 海豹
17. flipper 鰭狀肢
18. walrus 海象
19. tusk 海象的長牙
20. turtle 鱉
21. lobster 龍蝦
22. shrimp 小蝦
23. mussel 貽貝／蠔
24. crab 蟹
25. claw 爪
26. clam 蛤／蚌
27. starfish 海星

Which is the biggest – the <u>walrus</u>
or the <u>whale</u>?
The <u>whale</u> is the biggest.

Which is the biggest – the lobster, or the shrimp?
The .... is the biggest.

Which is the biggest – the clam or the starfish?
The .... is the biggest.

Which is the biggest – the shark or the angelfish?
....

1. flamingo 火鶴
2. pelican 鵜鶘
3. bill 鳥嘴
4. swan 天鵝
5. stork 鸛
6. crane 鶴
7. gull 鷗
8. duck 鴨
9. duckling 小鴨
10. penguin 企鵝
11. flipper 鰭狀肢
12. crow 烏鴉
13. ostrich 鴕鳥
14. eagle 鷹
15. beak 鳥嘴
16. hawk 鳶鷂
17. claw 鳥爪
18. owl 貓頭鷹
19. peacock 孔雀
20. feather 羽毛
21. pigeon 鴿
22. pheasant 雉
23. tail 尾
24. robin 知更鳥
25. blue jay 藍背樫鳥
26. hummingbird 蜂雀
27. wing 翼
28. swallow 燕子
29. cockatoo 大鸚鵡
30. crest 鳥冠
31. nest 鳥巢
32. egg 鳥蛋

Which do you like better, swans or peacocks?
I like swans <u>better</u>.

.........., penguin or stock?
.........., ostrich or flamingo?
.........., eagle or hawk?

A. Insects 昆蟲

1. bee 蜜蜂
2. honeycomb 蜂巢／蜂房
3. fly 蒼蠅
4. mosquito 蚊子
5. cockroach/roach 蟑螂
6. caterpillar 毛蟲
7. butterfly 蝴蝶
8. ladybug 瓢蟲
9. cricket 蟋蟀
10. ant 螞蟻
11. dragonfly 蜻蜓
12. spider* 蜘蛛

B. Rodents 齧齒類

13. rat 鼠
14. mouse 小鼠
15. squirrel 松鼠
16. chipmunk 花栗鼠

*not an insect

Is that a <u>bee</u> or <u>fly</u>? [1] It's a <u>bee</u>.

Is that a fly or a mosquito? [4] It's a ....
Is that a rat or a mouse? [14] It's a ....

Is that a squirrel or a chipmunk? [15] ....
Is that a caterpillar or a butterlfy? [6] ....

SPACE 太空

1. galaxy 星系／銀河系
2. star 星／恒星
3. comet 彗星
4. Sun 太陽
5. planet/Saturn 行星／土星
6. Earth 地球
7. Moon 月球
8. astronaut 太空人
9. space suit 太空衣
10. flag 旗
11. lunar module 登月艙
12. lunar vehicle 月球車
13. satellite 人造衛星
14. space shuttle 太空穿梭機
15. fuel tank 燃料箱
16. booster rocket
    火箭推進器／助推火箭

Have you every see a <u>galaxy</u>?	Yes, I have./No, I haven't.

Have you ever seen a space shuttle?   ....
Have you ever seen a lunar module?   ....

Have you every seen a planet?   ....
Have you ever seen a comet?   ....

THE MILITARY 軍隊

A. Army 陸軍
1. soldier 軍人
2. fatigues 戰鬥服
3. camouflage 偽裝
4. bayonet 刺刀
5. rifle 步槍
6. machine gun 機關槍
7. jeep 吉普車
8. cannon 火砲
9. tank 坦克車

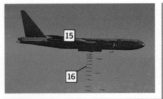
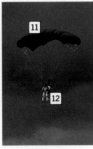

B. Air Force 空軍
10. pilot 飛行員
11. parachute 降落傘
12. parachutist 降傘者
13. helicopter 直升飛機
14. fighter plane 戰鬥機
15. bomber 轟炸機
16. bomb 炸彈

C. Navy 海軍
17. sailor 水兵
18. submarine 潛水艇
19. destroyer 驅逐艦
20. radar antenna 雷達天線
21. battleship 戰艦
22. aircraft carrier 航空母艦

D. Marines
海軍陸戰隊士兵

Was Jim ever <u>a soldier</u>?
Yes, he was./No, he wasn't.

Was Jim ever a pilot?
....

Was Jim ever a sailor?
....

A. Hobbies
愛好

1. coin collecting
   錢幣蒐集
2. coin 錢幣
3. (coin) album 集幣簿
4. coin catalog
   錢幣分類錄
5. magnifying glass
   放大鏡
6. stamp collecting
   集郵
7. (stamp) album
   集郵簿
8. stamp 郵票
9. stamp catalog
   郵票目錄
10. photography 攝影
11. camera 照相機
12. astronomy 天文學
13. telescope
    天文望遠鏡
14. bird watching
    野鳥觀察

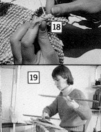

B. Crafts 手藝

15. sculpting 雕塑
16. sculpture 雕塑品
17. knitting 編織毛線
18. knitting needle
    編織毛線所用的
    長針
19. weaving 紡織
20. loom 織布機
21. pottery 陶器製造
22. potter's wheel
    製陶器用的轉盤
23. painting 繪畫
24. brush 畫筆
25. woodworking 木工

C. Games 遊戲

26. chess 國際象棋
27. board 棋盤
28. checkers 西洋棋
29. backgammon
    西洋雙陸棋
30. Scrabble 拼字遊戲
31. Monopoly
    大富翁遊戲
32. cards 撲克牌

Do you play <u>chess</u>?
Yes, I do./No, I don't, but I play <u>backgammon</u>.

Do you play checkers?   Do you play Scrabble?   Do you play Monopoly?   ....?
....

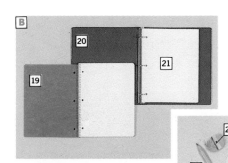

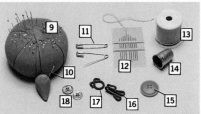

A. Sewing 縫紉

1. sewing machine 縫紉機
2. sewing basket 針綫籃
3. tape measure 捲尺
4. yarn 紗／線
5. knitting needle
   織毛線用的長針
6. (pair of) scissors 剪刀
7. zipper 拉鍊
8. material 布料
9. pin cushion 針包
10. straight pin 直針
11. safety pin 別針
12. needle 縫衣針
13. thread 線
14. thimble 頂針
15. button 鈕扣
16. hook 鈎
17. eye 眼
18. snap 子母扣

B. Sundries
日用雜物

19. (spiral) notebook 筆記簿
20. loose-leaf binder 活頁夾
21. (loose-leaf) paper 活頁紙
22. pencil 鉛筆
23. pencil sharpener
    鉛筆鉋／鉛筆刀
24. protractor 量角器
25. compass 圓規
26. wrapping paper 包裝紙
27. bow 蝶結
28. box 箱／盒
29. tissue paper 紙巾
30. ribbon 絲帶
31. string 細繩
32. masking tape
    不透光膠紙（油漆時遮蓋
    不上漆部分）

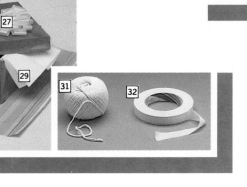

[22] Could I borrow a <u>pencil</u>?
Sure./Sorry. I don't have <u>one</u>.

[21] Could I borrow some <u>paper</u>?
Sure./Sorry. I don't have <u>any</u>.

[12] Could I borrow a ....?
....

[32] Could I borrow some ....?
....

[11] Could I borrow a ....?
....

[13] Could I borrow some ....?
....

a

accelerator / əkˈsɛləˌretɚ; əkˈseləreitə / 油門踏板 **55**-22

accessories / əkˈsɛsəriz; əkˈsesəriz / 配用品 **38**-D

accordion / əˈkɔrdɪən; əˈkɔːdiənll-ɔr- / 手風琴 **70**-21

action / ˈækʃən; ˈækʃən / 動作 **26**; **27**; **28**

actor / ˈæktɚ; ˈæktə / 男演員 **69**-12

actress / ˈæktrɪs; ˈæktris / 女演員 **69**-11

acute angle / əˌkjut ˈæŋgl; əˌkjuːt ˈæŋgəl ◀ / 銳角 **5**-8

address / əˈdrɛs; əˈdres / 地址 **19**-16

adhesive tape / ədˈhisɪv ˈtep; ədˌhiːsiv ˈteip◀ / 膠布 **29**-24

Afghanistan / æfˈgænəstæn; æfˈgænistaːn / 阿富汗 **8**

afraid / əˈfred; əˈfreid / 受驚 **32**-18

Africa / ˈæfrɪkə; ˈæfrikə / 非洲 **8**

after-shave (lotion) / ˈæftɚʃev ˌloʃən; ˈaːftəʃeiv ˌləuʃən / 鬍後水/刮鬍水 **25**-13

aircraft carrier / ˈɛrˌkræft kærɪɚ; ˈeəkraːft ˌkæriə / 航空母艦 **78**-22

air filter / ˈɛr ˌfɪltɚ; ˈeə ˌfiltə / 空氣過濾器 **55**-26

air force / ˈɛr fors; ˈeə fɔːs / 空軍 **78**-B

airport / ˈɛrˌport; ˈeəpɔːt / 機場 **59**; **60**

air tank / ˈɛr tæŋk; ˈeə tæŋk / 氣瓶 **63**-9

aisle / aɪl; ail / 通道 **69**-15

aisle seat / ˈaɪl sit; ˈail siːt / 靠通道坐位 **60**-33

Alabama / ˌæləˈbæmə; ˌæləˈbæmə / 阿拉巴馬 **9**

Alaska / əˈlæskə; əˈlæskə / 阿拉斯加 **9**

Albania / ælˈbenɪə; ælˈbeiniə / 阿爾巴尼亞 **8**

Alberta / ælˈbɝtə; ælˈbɜːtə / 亞伯達 **10**

album / ˈælbəm; ˈælbəm / 集幣簿/集郵簿 **79**-3, 7

Algeria / ælˈdʒɪrɪə; ælˈdʒiəriə / 阿爾及利亞 **8**

Alka Seltzer / ˌælkə ˈsɛltsɚ; ˌælkə ˈseltsə / 抗酸劑 **29**-20

alley / ˈælɪ; ˈæli / 保齡球場 **68**-37

alligator / ˈæləˌgetɚ; ˈæligeitə / 美洲鱷 **72**-32

alternator / ˈɔltɚˌnetɚ; ˈɔːltəneitə / 交流發電機 **55**-29

aluminium foil / əˈlumɪnɪəm fɔɪl; æljuˌminiəm ˈfɔil◀ / 鋁箔 **45**-30

a.m. / ˈeˌɛm; ei ˈem / 上午 **2**-i

amethyst / ˈæməˌθɪst; ˈæmiθist / 紫晶 **38**-21

amplifier / ˈæmpləˌfaɪɚ; ˈæmplifaiə / 放大器 **51**-9

analogue watch / ˈænəˌlɔg ˌwatʃ; ˈænəlog ˌwɔtʃ / 指針手錶 **2**-f

angelfish / ˈendʒəlfɪʃ; ˈeindʒəlfiʃ / 神仙魚 **74**-9

Angola / æŋˈgolə; æŋˈgəulə / 安哥拉 **8**

angry / ˈæŋgrɪ; ˈæŋgri / 憤怒 **32**-10

ankle / ˈæŋkl; ˈæŋkəl / 足踝 **23**-35

annoyed / əˈnɔɪd; əˈnɔid / 懊惱 **32**-12

answering machine / ˈænsərɪŋ məˈʃin; ˈaːnsəriŋ məˌʃiːn / 答話機/答錄機 **51**-21

ant / ænt; ænt / 螞蟻 **76**-10

antacid / æntˈæsɪd; æntˈæsid / 抗酸劑 **29**-20

Antarctica / æntˈarktɪkə; ænˈtaːktikə / 南極洲 **7**; **8**

antenna / ænˈtɛnə; ænˈtenə / 天綫 **39**-15

antler / ˈæntlɚ; ˈæntlə / 鹿角 **71**-23

apartment building / əˈpartmənt ˈbɪldɪŋ; əˈpaːtmənt ˈbildiŋ / 公寓大樓 **39**-D

apex / ˈepɛks; ˈeipeks / 頂點 **5**-9

Appalachian Mountains / ˌæpəˈletʃən ˈmauntnz; ˌæpəˈleitʃiən ˈmauntinz◀ / 阿帕拉契山脈 **9**

appetizers / ˈæpəˌtaɪzɚs; ˈæpitaizəs / 開胃藥 **17**-A

apple pie / ˈæpl ˈpaɪ; ˈæpəl ˈpai◀ / 蘋果餡餅 **17**-19

apples / ˈæpls; ˈæpəls / 蘋果 **15**-1

apricots / ˈeprɪˌkats; ˈeiprikɔts / 李/杏 **15**-12

April / ˈeprəl; ˈeiprəl / 四月 **3**

Arabian Sea / əˈrebɪən si; əˈreibiən ˈsi ◀ / 阿拉伯海 **8**

archer / ˈartʃɚ; ˈaːtʃə / 射箭者 **67**-13

archery / ˈartʃərɪ; ˈaːtʃəri / 射箭 **67**-E

architect / ˈarkəˌtɛkt; ˈaːkitekt / 建築師 **22**-36

Arctic Ocean / ˈarktɪk ˈoʃən; ˈaːktik ˈəuʃən / 北冰洋 **7**; **8**

Argentina / ˌardʒənˈtinə; aːdʒənˈtiːnə / 阿根廷 **7**

Arizona / ˌærəˈzonə; æriˈzəunə / 亞利桑那 **9**

Arkansas / ˈarkənsɔ; ˈaːkənsɔː / 阿肯色 **9**

arm / arm; aːm / 臂 **23**-11

armchair / ˈarmˌtʃɛr; ˈaːmtʃeə / 靠手椅 **42**-9

armrest / ˈarmrɛst; ˈaːmrest / 靠手 **60**-37

army / ˈarmɪ; ˈaːmi / 陸軍 **78**-A

arrival and departure board / əˈraɪvl ənd dɪˈpartʃɚ ˈbord; əˈraivəl ənd diˈpaːtʃə ˈbɔːd / 飛機到達及起飛指示牌/列車到站及離站顯示牌 **56**-4; **59**-4

arrow / ˈæro; ˈærəu / 箭 **67**-15

artery / ˈartərɪ; ˈaːtəri / 動脈 **24**-52

artichokes / ˈartɪˌtʃoks; ˈaːtitʃəuks / 朝鮮薊 **16**-20

artist / ˈartɪst; ˈaːtist / 畫家 **22**-46

ashamed / əˈʃemd; əˈʃeimd / 慚愧 **32**-15

Asia / ˈeʒə; ˈeiʃə / 亞洲 **8**

asparagus / əˈspærəgəs; əˈspærəgəs / 蘆筍/露筍 **16**-24

aspirin / ˈæspərɪn; ˈæsprin / 阿司匹靈 **29**-10

astronaut / ˈæstrəˌnɔt; ˈæstrənɔːt / 太空人 **77**-8

astronomy / əˈstranəmɪ; əˈstrɔnəmi / 天文學 **79**-12

Atlantic Ocean / ətˈlæntɪk ˈoʃən; ətˌlæntik ˈəuʃn / 大西洋 **7**; **8**; **9**; **10**

attaché case / ˌætəˈʃe kes; əˈtæʃei keis / 公文提箱/手提箱 **38**-27

attendant / əˈtɛndənt; əˈtendənt / 服務員 **55**-5

audience / ˈɔdɪəns; ˈɔːdiəns / 觀眾 **69**-14

audio cassette / ˈɔdɪo kæˈsɛt; ˈɔːdiəu kəˈset / 錄音帶 **51**-20

August / ˈɔgəst; ˈɔːgəst / 八月 **3**

aunt / ænt; aːnt / 舅母 **31**

Australia / ɔˈstreljə; ɔˈstreiliə / 澳洲 **8**

Austria / ˈɔstrɪə; ˈɔstriə / 奧地利 **8**

automatic teller / ˌɔtəˈmætɪk ˈtɛlɚ; ɔːtəˈmætik◀ ˈtelə / 自動提款機 **6**-8

avocados / ˌavəˈkadoz; ævəˈkaːdəuz◀ / 鱷梨/牛油果 **15**-7

awl / ɔl; ɔːl / 錐子 **40**-24

azalea / əˈzeljə; əˈzeiliə / 杜鵑花 **40**-21

b

baby / ˈbebɪ; ˈbeibi / 嬰兒 **47**-21

baby bottle / ˈbebɪ ˈbatl; ˈbeibi ˈbɔtl / 奶瓶 **47**-21

baby carrier / ˈbebɪ ˈkærɪɚ; ˈbeibi ˈkæriə / 嬰兒背帶 **47**-13

baby chair / ˈbebɪ ˈtʃɛr; ˈbeibi tʃeə / 兒童椅 **47**-9

baby clothes / ˈbebɪ ˈkloz; beibi ˈkləuðz / 嬰兒服裝 **47**-24

baby seat / ˈbebɪ ˈsit; ˈbeibi ˈsiːt / 嬰兒座位 **47**-18

back / bæk; bæk / 背 **23**-26

backboard / ˈbækbord; ˈbækbɔːd / 籃板 **66**-42

backgammon / ˈbækgæmən; ˈbækgæmən / 西洋雙陸棋 **79**-29

backhoe / ˈbækho; ˈbækhəu / 挖土機 **53**-12

backpack / ˈbækpæk; ˈbækpæk / 背囊 **67**-23

backyard / ˈbækjard; ˈbækjaːd / 後院 **40**

bacon / ˈbekən; ˈbeikən / 煙肉 **14**-20

bad / bæd; bæd / 壞 **33**-12

Baffin Bay / ˈbæfɪn ˈbe; ˈbæfin ˈbei / 巴芬灣 **7**-10

Baffin Island / ˈbæfɪn ˈaɪlənd; ˈbæfin ˈailənd / 巴芬島 **10**

bag / bæg; bæg / 袋子 **13**-7

baggage claim area / ˈbægɪdʒ klem ˈɛrɪə; ˈbægidʒ kleim ˈeəriə / 行李領取處 **59**-12

baggage claim check / ˈbægɪdʒ klem tʃɛk; ˈbægidʒ kleim tʃek / 行李領取單 **59**-17

Bahamas / bəˈhaməz; bəˈhaːməz / 巴哈馬 **7**

Bahrain / baˈren; baːˈrein / 巴林島 **8**

doll / dɑl; dɔl / 玩偶 **48**-15

dollar / 'dɑlɚ; 'dɔlə / 一元 **6**-25

dollar bill / 'dɑlɚ bɪl; 'dɔlə bil / 一美元鈔票 **6**-25

doll carriage / 'dɑl 'kærɪdʒ; 'dɔl 'kærɪdʒ / 玩具車 **48**-16

dolphin / 'dɑlfɪn; 'dɔlfin / 海豚 **74**-15

Dominican Republic / də'mɪnɪkən rɪ'pʌblɪk; də'minikən ri'pʌblik / 多米尼加共和國 **7**

do not enter sign / du nɑt ɛntɚ saɪn; du: nɔt entə sain / 不准駛入標誌 **58**-29

donut / 'donʌt; 'dəunʌt / 炸餅圈/甜甜圈 **18**-18

door / dor; dɔːr / 車門 **56**-19

door handle / 'dor 'hændl; 'dɔː 'hændl / 門把手 **45**-25; **56**-18

doorknob / 'dor,nɑb; 'dɔːnɔb / 球形門把手 **39**-13; **44**-12

double boiler / 'dʌbl 'bɔɪlɚ; 'dʌbəl 'bɔilə / 雙層蒸鍋 **46**-1

double yellow lines / 'dʌbl jɛlo 'laɪns; 'dʌbəl jeləu 'lains / 雙黃線 **58**-20

downhill skiing / ˌdaʊnhɪl 'ski-ɪŋ; ˌdaunhil 'ski-iŋ / 滑雪下山 **64**-B

downstairs apartment / ˌdaʊnstɛrz ə'partmənt; ˌdaunsteəz əpɑ:tmənt / 樓下住宅 **39**-17

dargonfly / 'dræɡənflaɪ; 'dræɡənflai / 蜻蜓 **76**-11

drape / drep; dreip / 窗簾 **41**-14

draw / drɔ; drɔː / 畫 **28**-13

drawer / drɔr; drɔː / 抽屜 **43**-10; **45**-23

dress / drɛs; dres / 連衣裙/洋裝 **36**-A; **6**

dresser / 'drɛsɚ; 'dresə / 梳妝枱 **43**-13

drill / drɪl; dril / 鑽子 **30**-3

drink / drɪŋk; driŋk / 飲/喝 **26**-14

driver / 'draɪvɚ; 'draivə / 司機 **56**-12

driveway / 'draɪvwe; 'draivwei / 車道 **39**-1

drum / drʌm; drʌm / 鼓 **70**-18

dry / draɪ; drai / 乾 **33**-22

dry off / draɪ ɔf; drai 'ɔf / 抹乾 **26**-4

dryer / 'draɪɚ; 'draiə / 乾衣機/烘衣機 **49**-16

duck / dʌk; dʌk / 鴨 **75**-8

duckling / 'dʌklɪŋ; 'dʌkliŋ / 小鴨 **75**-9

dump truck / 'dʌmp trʌk; 'dʌmp trʌk / 傾卸車 **53**-10

dune / djun; dju:n / 沙丘 **54**-18

duplex / 'djuplɛks; 'dju:pleks / 兩戶複式住宅 **39**-C

dust / dʌst; dʌst / 抹 **26**-16

dust cloth / dʌst klɔθ; dʌst klɔθ / 抹布 **49**-4

dust mop / dʌst mɑp; dʌst mɑp / 撣塵拖把 **49**-11

dustpan / 'dʌst,pæn; 'dustpæn / 簸箕 **49**-5

dust ruffle / dʌst ,rʌfl; dʌst ,rʌfəl / 縐邊牀裙/牀幕 **43**-6

e

eagle / 'iɡl; 'i:ɡəl / 鷹 **75**-14

ear / ɪr; iə / 耳朵 **23**-4

earring / 'ɪr,rɪŋ; 'iə,riŋ / 耳環 **38**-6

Earth / ɝθ; ɜ:θ / 地球 **77**-6

east / ist; i:st / 東 **9**

East / ist; i:st / 東部 **9**

East China Sea / ist ,tʃaɪnə 'si; i:st ,tʃainə 'si: / 東海 **8**

Easter / 'istɚ; 'i:stə / 復活節 **3**-5

East Germany / ist 'dʒɝmənɪ; i:st 'dʒɜ:məni / 東德 **8**

eat / it; i:t / 吃 **26**-13

ecstatic / ɪk'stætɪk; ik'stætik / 狂喜 **32**-3

Ecuador / 'ɛkwədɔr; 'ekwədɔ: / 厄瓜多爾 **7**

edge / ɛdʒ; edʒ / 邊緣 **5**-4

eel / il; i:l / 鰻/鱔 **74**-11

egg / ɛɡ; eɡ / 鳥蛋 **75**-32

egg beater / 'ɛɡ 'bitɚ; 'eɡ 'bi:tə / 打蛋器 **46**-23

egg plants / 'ɛɡ plænts; 'eɡ plɑ:nts / 茄子/矮瓜 **16**-22

eggs / ɛɡs; eɡs / 蛋類 **13**-14

Egypt / 'idʒɪpt; 'i:dʒipt / 埃及 **8**

El Salvador / ɛl 'sælvə,dor; el 'sælvə,dɔ: / 薩爾瓦多 **7**

elbow / 'ɛl,bo; 'elbəu / 手肘 **23**-29

electric blanket / ɪ,lɛktrɪk 'blæŋkɪt; i,lektrik 'blæŋkit / 電毯 **43**-19

electric drill / ɪ,lɛktrɪk 'drɪl; i,lektrik 'dril / 電鑽 **50**-29

electrician / ɪ,lɛk'trɪʃən; i,lek'triʃən / 電工 **21**-10

electric mixer / ɪ,lɛk'rɪk 'mɪksɚ; i,lektrik 'miksə / 電攪拌器 **46**-20

electric pencil sharpener / ɪ,lɛktrɪk pɛnsl 'ʃɑrpənɚ; i,lek'trik pensəl 'ʃɑ:pənə / 電動鉛筆鉋 **20**-5

electric shaver / ɪ'lɛktrɪk ʃevɚ; i,lektrik 'ʃeivə / 電刮鬍刀 **25**-23

electric typewriter / ɪ,lɛktrɪk 'taɪpraɪtɚ; i,lektrik 'taipraitə / 電動打字機 **52**-36

electronics / ɪ,lɛk'trɑnɪks; i,lek'trɔniks / 電子工業產品 **51**-52

electronic typewriter / ɪ,lɛktrɑnɪk 'taɪpraɪtɚ; ilek,trɔnik ,taipraitə / 電子打字機 **52**-35

elephant / 'ɛləfənt; 'elifənt / 象 **71**-8

elevator / 'ɛlə,vetɚ; 'eliveitə / 電梯 **39**-21

ellipse / ɪ'lɪps; i'lips / 橢圓形 **5**-G

embarrassed / ɪm'bærəst; im,bærəst / 感困窘 **32**-14

emerald / 'ɛmərəld; 'emərəld / 綠寶石 **38**-24

emery board / 'ɛmrɪ 'bord; 'eməri 'bɔ:d / 砂板 **25**-19

emotions / ɪ'moʃəns; i'məuʃəns / 情緒 **32**

empty / 'ɛmptɪ; 'empti / 空 **34**-32

end table / ,ɛnd 'tebl; end 'teibəl / 茶几 **41**-7

engine / 'ɛndʒən; 'endʒin / 發動機 **55**-28

entertainment / ,ɛntɚtenmənt; ,entə'teinmənt / 娛樂 **69**

entrées / 'ɑntre; 'ɔntrei / 主餐/正菜 **17**-C

envelope / 'ɛnvə,lop; 'envələup / 信封 **19**-14

equals / 'ikwəlz; 'i:kwəlz / 等於 **1**

erase / ɪ'res; i'reiz / 擦掉/抹去 **28**-3

eraser / ɪ'resɚ; i'reizə / 橡皮擦 **20**-27

Ethiopia / iθɪ'opɪə; ,i:θi'əupiə / 衣索比亞 **8**

Europe / 'jurəp; 'juərəp / 歐洲 **8**

exact exchange lane / ɪɡ'zækt ɪks,tʃɛndʒ len; iɡ'zækt iks,tʃeindʒ lein / 不找零錢車道 **57**-15

excavation site / ,ɛkskə'veʃən saɪt; ekskə'veiʃən ,sait / 挖掘區 **53**-9

exit / 'ɛɡzɪt; 'eɡzit / 出口 **12**-26

express mail / ɪk'sprɛs mel; ik'spres meil / 快郵 **19**-4

extension cord / ɪk'stɛnʃən kɔrd; ik'stenʃən kɔ:d / 拖線 **49**-29

eye / aɪ; ai / 眼睛/眼 **23**-3; **80**-17

eyebrow / 'aɪ,braʊ; 'aibrau / 眉毛 **24**-42

eyebrow pencil / 'aɪbraʊ 'pɛnsl; 'aibrau 'pensəl / 眉筆 **25**-4

eyelash / 'aɪlæʃ; ailæʃ / 睫毛 **24**-44

eyelid / 'aɪ,lɪd; 'ailid / 眼瞼/眼皮 **24**-43

eyeliner / 'aɪ,laɪnɚ; 'ai,lainə / 眼線筆 **25**-5

eye shadow / 'aɪ,ʃædo; 'ai ʃædəu / 眼影 **25**-7

f

face / fes; feis / 鐘面/臉 **2**-d; **23**-1

Falkland Islands / 'fɔlklænd ,aɪləndz; 'fɔ:klənd ,ailəndz / 福克蘭羣島 **7**

fall / fɔl; fɔ:l / 秋季/跌 **4**-2; **28**-23

family / fæməlɪ; 'fæməli / 家庭 **31**

farm / farm; fɑ:m / 農場 **73**

farmer / farmɚ; fɑ:mə / 農夫 **21**-16; **73**-11

farmhouse / 'farmhaʊs; 'fɑrmhaʊs / 農舍 **73**-2

farmland / 'farmlænd; 'fɑ:mlænd / 農田 **73**-1

fast / fæst; fɑ:st / 快 **34**-25

fast foods / fæst fudz; 'fɑ:st fu:dz / 快餐 **18**

father / 'faðɚ; 'fɑ:ðə / 父親 **31**

father-in-law / 'faðɚ ɪn lɔ; 'fɑ:ðər in lɔ: / 岳父/公公 **31**

g

Georgia / ˈdʒɔrdʒə; ˈdʒɔːdʒə / 喬治亞洲 **9**

geranium / dʒəˈrɛniəm; dʒəˈreiniəm / 天竺葵 **40**-24

gerbil / ˈdʒɜrbl; ˈdʒɜːbəl / 沙鼠 **72**-46

get dressed / gɛt ˈdrɛst; get ˈdrest / 穿衣 **26**-7

get up / gɛt ˈʌp; get ˈʌp / 起床 **26**-2

Ghana / ˈgænə; ˈgɑːnə / 迦納 **8**

gill / gɪl; gil / 鰓 **74**-8

ginger / ˈdʒɪndʒər; ˈdʒindʒə / 薑 **16**-27

giraffe / dʒəˈræf; dʒiˈrɑːf / 長頸鹿 **71**-21

girder / ˈgɜrdər; ˈgɜːdə / 樑 **53**-3

give / gɪv; giv / 給 **28**-4

glove / glʌv; glʌv / 手套 **37**-5; **65**-25; **66**-52, 67; **68**-45

go down / go daʊn; gəʊ daʊn / 向下走 **28**-22

go to bed / go tʊ bɛd; gəʊ tə bed / 上床 **26**-21

go up / go ʌp; gəʊ ʌp / 向上走 **28**-19

goal / gol; gəʊl / 球門 **66**-45, 49

goalie / ˈgolɪ; ˈgəʊli / 守門員 **66**-50

goat / got; ˈgəʊt / 山羊 **73**-26

gold / gold; gəʊld / 金 **38**-17

goldfish / ˈgoldfɪʃ; ˈgəʊldfiʃ / 金魚 **72**-51

golf / gɔlf; gɔlf / 打高爾夫球 **67**-F

golf ball / gɔlf bol; ˈgɔlf boːl / 高爾夫球 **67**-19

golf club / gɔlf klʌb; ˈgɔlf klʌb / 球桿 **67**-18

golfer / ˈgɔlfər; ˈgɔlfə / 打高爾夫球者 **67**-17

good / gʊd; gʊd / 好 **33**-11

gorilla / gəˈrɪlə; gəˈrɪle / 大猩猩 **71**-29

Grand Canyon / ˌgrænd ˈkænjən; ˌgrænd ˈkænjən / 大峽谷 **9**

grandchildren / ˈgrændˌtʃɪldrən; ˈgrænˌtʃildrən / 孫子女 **31**

granddaughter / ˈgrændɔtər; ˈgrænˌdɔːtə / 孫女 **31**

grandfather / ˈgrænˌfɑðər; ˈgrænˌfɑːðə / 祖父 **31**

grandmother / ˈgrænˌmʌðər; ˈgrænˌmʌðə / 祖母 **31**

grandparents / ˈgrænˌpɛrənts; ˈgrænˌpeərənts / 祖父母 **31**

grandson / ˈgrænˌsʌn; ˌgrænsʌn / 孫子 **31**

grapefruitsl / ˈgrepˌfruts; ˈgreipfruːts / 西柚/葡萄柚 **15**-15

grapes / grepz; ˈgreipz / 葡萄 **15**-3

grass / græs; grɑːs / 草坪/草 **40**-3; **54**-7

grater / ˈgretər; ˈgreitə / 擦板 **46**-27

gray / gre; grei / 綠 **35**-22

Great Britain / gret ˈbrɪtən; greit ˈbritən / 大不列顛 **8**

Great Salt Lake / gret ˈsɔlt lek; greit ˈsɔlt leik / 大鹽湖 **9**

Greece / gris; griːs / 希臘 **8**

green / grin; griːn / 綠/果嶺 **35**-23; **67**-21

green beans / grin bins; griːn biːns / 扁豆/四季豆 **16**-21; **17**-15

Greenland / ˈgrinlənd; ˈgriːnlənd / 格陵蘭 **7**

Greenland Sea / ˌgrinlənd si; ˌgriːnlənd siː / 格陵蘭海 **8**

green onions / grin ʌnjənz; griːn ʌnjənz / 葱 **16**-2

green peppers / grin pɛpəz; griːn pepəz / 青燈籠椒 **16**-9

grieving / grivɪŋ; griːviŋ / 哀傷 **32**-8

grocer / ˈgrosər; ˈgrəʊsə / 食品雜貨商 **13**-5

groceries / ˈgrosərɪz; ˈgrəʊsəriz / 食品雜貨 **13**-5

ground meat / ˌgraʊnd ˈmit; ˌgraʊnd miːt / 碎肉 **14**-24

Guatemala / gwætəˈmalə; gwɑːtəˈmɑːlə / 瓜地瑪拉 **7**

guest towel / ˈgɛst taʊl; ˈgest taʊəl / 客用毛巾 **44**-1

Guinea / ˈgɪnɪ; ˈgini / 幾內亞 **8**

Guinea Bissau / ˌgɪnɪbɪsau; ˌginibiˈsaʊ / 幾內亞比紹 **8**

guinea pig / ˈgɪnɪ pɪg; ˈgini pig / 天竺鼠 **72**-49

guitar / gɪˈtar; giˈtɑː / 吉他/大弦琴 **70**-6

Gulf of Mexico / ˌgʌlf əv ˈmɛksɪko; ˌgʌlf əv ˈmeksikəʊ / 墨西哥灣 **7**; **9**

gull / gʌl; gʌl / 鷗 **75**-7

gum / gʌm; gʌm / 口香糖/香口膠 **18**-17

gutter / gʌtər; gʌtə / 排水溝/屋坑 **39**-7; **68**-36

Guyana / gaɪˈænə; gaiˈænə / 蓋那亞 **7**

gym / dʒɪm; dʒim / 健身房 **27**

h

hair / hɛr; heə / 頭髮 **23**-2

hair brush / hɛr brʌʃ; heə brʌʃ / 髮刷 **25**-21

hairdresser / ˈhɛrˌdrɛsər; ˈheəˌdresə / 美容師 **22**-40

hair dryer / ˈhɛrˌdraɪər; ˈheəˌdraiə / 吹風器 **25**-22

hair tonic / ˈhɛr ˌtɑnɪk; ˈheə ˌtɔnik / 生髮水 **25**-14

Haiti / ˈheti; ˈheiti / 海地 **7**

half / hæf; hɑːf / 一半 **1**

halfback / ˈhæfˌbæk; ˈhɑːfbæk / 中衛 **65**-29

half dollar / hæf dalər; hɑːf dɔlə / 五角硬幣 **6**-23

half slip / hæf slɪp; hɑːf slip / 底/襯裙 **36**-15

hall / hol; hɔːl / 門廳 **39**-25

Halloween / ˌhæloˈin; ˌhæləʊiːn / 萬聖節前夕 **3**-11

hamburger / ˈhæmbɜɡər; ˈhæmbɜːgə / 漢堡飽 **18**-24

hammer / ˈhæmər; ˈhæmə / 鎚 **50**-12

hamper / ˈhæmpər; ˈhæmpə / 有蓋提籃 **49**-20

hamster / ˈhæmstər; ˈhæmstə / 倉鼠 **72**-48

hand / ˈhænd; hænd / 手 **23**-14

handbag / ˈhændbæg; ˈhændbæg / 女用手提包 **36**-5

handball / ˈhændˌbɔl; ˈhændbɔːl / 手球 **68**-M

handball player / ˈhændbɔl pleə; ˈhændbɔːl pleiə / 打手球者 **68**-44

hand beater / ˈhænd bitər; hænd biːtə / 打蛋器 **46**-23

hand drill / ˈhænd drɪl; ˈhænd dril / 手鑽 **50**-31

handkerchief / ˈhæŋkətʃɪf; ˈhæŋkətʃif / 手帕 **38**-31

handle / ˈhændl; ˈhændl / 手柄/把手/鍋柄/(門)把手 **43**-11; **45**-25; **46**-6; **56**-18

hand towel / ˈhænd ˌtaʊl; hænd ˌtaʊəl / 抹手毛布 **44**-3

hangar / ˈhæŋər; ˈhæŋə / 機庫 **60**-47

hanger / ˈhæŋər; ˈhæŋə / 衣架 **49**-25

happy / ˈhæpɪ; ˈhæpi / 高興 **32**-2

harbor / ˈharbər; ˈhɑːbə / 海港 **61**-1

hard / hard; hɑːd / 硬 **34**-44

hard hat / ˈhard hæt; ˈhɑːd hæt / 安全帽 **53**-5

harmonica / harˈmanɪkə; hɑːˈmɔnikə / 口琴 **70**-22

hat / hæt; hæt / 帽子/遮陽帽 **37**-4; **62**-15

hatchet / ˈhætʃɪt; ˈhætʃit / 短柄小斧 **50**-33

Hawaii / hæˈwaɪ-ɪ; həˈwai-i / 夏威夷 **9**

hawk / hɔk; hɔːk / 鷹 **75**-16

head / hɛd; hed / 頭 **23**-24

headache / ˈhɛdˌek; ˈhedeik / 頭痛 **29**-9

headboard / ˈhɛdˈbɔrd; ˈhedbɔːd / 牀頭板 **43**-2

headphone / ˈhɛdˌfon; ˈhedfəʊn / 耳筒 **51**-19

heart / hart; hɑːt / 心臟/心 **24**-56

heat control / hit kənˈtrol; hiːt kənˈtrəʊl / (熱)調節器 **43**-20

heater / ˈhitər; ˈhiːtə / 加熱器 **55**-19

heater hose / hitər hoz; hiːtə həʊz / 加熱器軟管 **55**-25

heavy / ˈhɛvɪ; ˈhevi / 重 **33**-8

hedge / hɛdʒ; hedʒ / 樹籬 **40**-14

heel / hil; hiːl / 踵/後跟 **23**-36; **37**-14

height / haɪt; hait / 高度 **5**-6

helicopter / ˈhɛlɪˌkaptər; ˈhelikɔptə / 直昇機 **60**-46; **78**-13

helmet / ˈhɛlmɪt; helmit / 頭盔/防護帽 **64**-17; **65**-21; **67**-4

hen / hɛn; hen / 小雞/母雞 **73**-28

hero / ˈhɪro; ˈhiərəʊ / 大型三明治/三文治 **18**-1

high / haɪ; hai / 高 **33**-3

high chair / ˈhaɪ tʃɛr; ˈhai tʃeə / 嬰兒高椅 **47**-16

highway / ˈhaɪˌwe; ˈhaiwei / 公路 **57**-A

hiker / ˈhaɪkər; ˈhaikə / 徒步旅行者 **67**-22

hiking / ˈhaɪkɪŋ; ˈhaikiŋ / 徒步旅行 **67**-G

hiking boot / ˈhaɪkɪŋ ˈbut; ˈhaikiŋ ˈbuːt / 步行靴 **67**-24

l

Labor Day / 'lebɚ de; 'leibə dei / 勞動節 **3**-10

Labrador Sea / 'læbrə،dɔr si; 'læbrədɔ:(r) si: / 拉布拉多海 **10**

ladder / 'lædɚ; 'lædə / 梯 **53**-4

ladle / 'ledl; 'leidl / 長柄杓子 **46**-22

ladybug / 'ledɪˌbʌg; 'leidibʌg / 瓢蟲 **76**-8

lake / lek; leik / 湖 **54**-12

Lake Erie / lek 'ɪrɪ; leik 'iəri / 伊利湖 **9**

Lake Huron / lek 'hjurən; leik 'hjʊərn / 休倫湖 **9**

Lake Michigan / lek 'mɪʃɪgən; leik 'miʃigən / 密西根湖 **9**

Lake Ontario / lek an'tɛrɪo; leik ɔn'teəriʊ / 安大略湖 **9**

Lake Superior / lek sə'pɪrɪɚ; leik su:'piəriə / 蘇必略湖 **9**

lamb / læm; læm / 小羊 **73**-25

lamb chops / læm tʃaps; læm tʃɔps / 羊排 **14**-26

lamp / læmp; læmp / 燈 **20**-2; **41**-8; **43**-8; **47**-6

lamp shade / 'læmp ʃed; 'læmp ʃeid / 燈罩 **41**-9

land / lænd; lænd / 陸地 **54**

Laos / lauz; lauz / 寮國 **8**

lapel / lə'pɛl; lə'pel / 翻領 **35**-4

large intestine / lardʒ ɪn'tɛstɪn; lɑːdʒ in'testin / 大腸 **24**-60

laugh / læf; lɑːf / 大笑 **28**-15

laundry / 'lɔndrɪ; 'lɔːndri / 要洗或已洗的衣服 **49**-19

laundry bag / 'lɔndrɪ bæg; 'lɔːndri bæg / 髒衣服袋 **49**-21

laundry basket / 'lɔndrɪ bæskɪt; 'lɔːndri bɑːskit / 髒衣服籃 **49**-22

laundry room / 'lɔndrɪ rum; 'lɔːdri ru:m / 洗衣房 **49**

lawn / lɔn; lɔːn / 草坪 **39**-11; **40**-3

lawn mower / 'lɔn moɚ; 'lɔːn məʊə / 割草機 **40**-4

leaf / lif; li:f / 樹葉 **40**-2

Lebanon / 'lɛbənən; 'lebənən / 黎巴嫩 **8**

leeks / likz; li:kz / 大蔥 **16**-30

left end / lɛft ɛnd; left end / 左翼 **65**-38

left guard / lɛft gard; left gɑːd / 左衛 **65**-36

left lane / lɛft len; left lein / 左車道 **57**-7

left tackle / lɛft tækl; left tækəl / 左擒拿手 **65**-

leg / lɛg; leg / 腿 **23**-18

lemons / 'lɛmənz; 'lemənz / 檸檬 **15**-13

length / lɛŋθ / 長度 **5**-15

lens / lɛnz; lenz / 鏡頭 **52**-

leopard / 'lɛpɚd; 'lepəd / 豹 **71**-6

Lesotho / lə'soto; lə'su:tu: / 萊索托 **8**

letter carrier / lɛtɚ kærɪɚ; letə kæriə / 郵差 **21**-14

lettuce / 'lɛtɪs; 'letis / 萵苣/生菜 **16**-1

level / 'lɛvl; 'levəl / 水平儀 **50**-27; **53**-18

Liberia / laɪ'bɪrɪə lai'biəriə / 賴比瑞亞 **8**

license plate / laɪsns plet; laisəns pleit / 車牌 **55**-8

lid / lɪd; lid / 鍋蓋 **46**-2

lie down / laɪ 'daun; lai 'daʊn / 躺下 **27**-4

lifeguard / laɪfgard; laifgɑːd / 救生員 **62**-11

lifeguard stard / laɪfgard stænd; laifgɑːd stænd / 救生員瞭望台 **62**-10

life jacket / laɪf dʒækɪt; laif dʒækit / 救生衣 **63**-34

lift / lɪft; lift / 舉起 **27**-14

light / laɪt; lait / 輕/光亮/門廊燈 **33**-7; **34**-35; **39**-

light switch / 'laɪt swɪtʃ; 'lait switʃ / 電燈開關 **44**-10

limes / laɪmz; laimz / 青檸 **15**-14

line / laɪn; lain / 釣絲/纜 **61**-12; **63**-13

Lines / laɪnz; lainz / 線 **5**-J

lion / laɪən; laiən / 獅 **71**-1

lip / lɪp; lip / 咀唇 **23**-7

lipstick / 'lɪpstɪk; 'lipstik / 唇膏/口紅 **25**-8

listen / 'lɪsn; 'lisən / 聽 **26**-18

liver / 'lɪvɚ; 'livə / 肝臟 **24**-57

living room / 'lɪvɪŋ rum; 'liviŋ ru:m / 客廳 **39**-30; **41**

lizard / 'lɪzɚd; 'lizəd / 蜥蜴 **72**-25

llama / 'lamə; 'lɑːmə / 駱馬 **71**-24

loafer / 'lofɚ; 'ləʊfə / 懶人鞋 **37**-17

lobby / 'labɪ; 'lɔbi / 走廊 **39**-20

lobster / 'labstɚ; 'lɔbstə / 龍蝦 **74**-21

long / lɔŋ; lɔŋ / 長 **33**-9

longshoreman / 'lɔŋˌʃormən; 'lɔŋʃɔːmən / 碼頭裝卸工人 **61**-14

loom / lum; lu:m / 織布機 **79**-20

loose / lus; lu:s / 鬆 **33**-5

loose-leaf binder / lus lif baɪndɚ; lu:s li:f baidə / 活頁夾 **80**-20

loose-leaf paper / lus lif pepɚ; lu:s li:f peipə / 活頁紙 **80**-21

Louisiana / luˌizɪ'ænə; lu:ˌi:zi'ænə / 路易西安那 **9**

lounge chair / laundʒ tʃɛr; laʊndʒ tʃeə / 躺椅 **40**-5; **62**-9

love seat / lʌv sit; lʌv si:t / 鴛鴦椅 **41**-5

low / lo; ləʊ / 低 **33**-4

luggage / 'lʌgɪdʒ; 'lʌgidʒ / 行李 **59**-15

luggage carousel / 'lʌgɪdʒ kærəˌzɛl; 'lʌgidʒ kærəˌsel / 行李旋轉輸送機 **59**-16

luggage carrier / 'lʌgɪdʒ kærɪɚ; 'lʌgidʒ kæriə / 行李車 **59**-14

luggage compartment / 'lʌgɪdʒ kəm'partmənt; 'lʌgidʒ kəmˌpɑ:tmənt / 行李格箱 **56**-14

lunar module / ˌlunɚ 'madʒul; ˌlu:nə 'mɔdju:l / 登月艙 **77**-11

lunar vehicle / ˌlunɚ 'vɪrkl; ˌlu:nə 'vi:ikəl / 月球車 **77**-12

lung / lʌŋ; lʌŋ / 肺 **24**-55

m

macaroni / ˌmækə'ronɪ; ˌmækə'rəʊni / 通心粉 **14**-31

machine gun / mə'ʃin gʌn; mə'ʃi:n gʌn / 機關槍 **78**-6

Mackenzie Mountains / mə'kɛnzɪ mauntnz; mə'kenzi maʊntinz / 馬更些山脈 **10**

Mackenzie River / mə'kɛnzɪ rɪvɚ; mə'kenzi rivə / 馬更些河 **10**

mad / mæd; mæd / 憤怒 **32**-10

Madagascar / mædə'gæskɚ; mædə'gæskə(r) / 馬達加斯加 **8**

magnifying glass / 'mægnəˌfaɪ-ɪŋ glas; 'mægnifai-iŋ glɑ:s / 放大鏡 **79**-5

mailbag / 'mel،bæg; 'meilbæg / 郵袋 **19**-8

mailbox / 'mel،baks; 'meilbɔks / 郵筒/郵箱 **19**-9; **39**-18

mail carrier / mel kærɪɚ; meil kæriə / 郵差 **19**-7

mail slot / mel slat; meil slɔt / 信箱入信口 **19**-5

mail truck / mel trʌk; meil trʌk / 郵箱 **19**-6

main courses / men korzɪs; mein kɔrzis / 正菜 **17**-C

Maine / men; mein / 緬因 **9**

Malawi / mələwi; mə'la:wi / 馬拉威 **8**

Malaysia / mə'leʒ(ɪ); mə'leiziə / 馬來西亞 **8**

Mali / 'malɪ; 'ma:li / 馬利 **8**

mane / men; mein / 鬃 **71**-2; **73**-17

mangoes / 'mæŋgoz; 'mæŋgəʊz / 芒果 **15**-5

Manitoba / ˌmænə'tobə; ˌmæni'təʊbə / 曼尼托巴 **10**

mantel / 'mæntl; 'mæntl / 壁爐架 **41**-21

March / martʃ; ma:tʃ / 三月 **3**

margarine / 'mardʒəˌrin; ˌma:dʒə'ri:n / 人造奶油/牛油 **13**-15

marines / mə'rins; mə'ri:ns / 海軍陸戰隊士兵 **78**-D

Maritime Provinces / mærətaɪm pravɪnsɪz; mæritaim prɔvinsiz / 沿海各省 **10**

marquee / mar'ki; ma:'ki: / 戲院外之遮簷 **69**-19

Maryland / 'mɛrələnd; 'meərilənd / 馬里蘭 **9**

mascara / mæs'kærə; mæs'ka:rə / 睫毛液 **25**-6

mask / mæsk; ma:sk / 面罩 **63**-10; **65**-24; -

masking tape / mæskɪŋ tep; ma:skiŋ teip / 不透光膠紙 **80**-32

mason / 'mesn; 'meisən / 砌磚工/泥水匠 **21**-2

Massachusetts / mæsə'ʃusəts; mæsə'tʃu:s / 馬薩諸塞州 **9**

west / wɛst; west / 西 **9**

West Coast / wɛst 'kost; west 'kəʊst / 西海岸 **9**

Western Canada / wɛstən 'kænədə; westən 'kænədə / 加拿大西部 **10**

Western Sahara / wɛstən sə'harə; westən sə'ha:rə / 撒哈拉西部 **8**

West Germany / wɛst 'dʒɜməni; west 'dʒɜ:mni / 西德 **8**

West Virginia / wɛst və'dʒɪnɪə; west və'dʒɪnɪə / 西維吉尼亞 **9**

wet / wɛt; wet / 濕 **33**-21

wet mop / 'wɛt map; 'wet mɔp / 濕水拖把 **49**-12

wet suit / 'wɛt sut; 'wet su:t / 潛泳衣 **63**-8

whale / hwel; weil / 鯨 **74**-14

wheat field / hwit fild; wi:t fi:ld / 麥田 **73**-8

wheel / hwil; wi:l / 輪 **67**-7

wheelbarrow / 'hwilbæro; 'wi:lbærəʊ / 手推車 **53**-19

whisk / hwɪsk; wisk / 打蛋器 **46**-28

whisk broom / hwɪsk brum; wisk bru:m / 小掃帚 / 掃把 **49**-6

whiskers / 'hwɪskər; 'wiskəz / 鬚 **72**-43

white / hwaɪt; wait / 白 **35**-24

white water rafting / hwaɪt wɑtər ræftɪŋ; wait wɔtə ra:ftɪŋ / 划橡皮艇過激流 **63**-M

wide / waɪd; waid / 寬 **34**-39

wide receiver / waɪd rɪ'si:vər; waid ri'si:və / 右翼 **65**-30, 38

width / wɪdθ; widθ / 濶度 **5**-14

wife / waɪf; waif / 妻子 **31**

winch / wɪntʃ; wintʃ / 絞車 **61**-11

window / 'wɪndo; 'windəʊ / 窗 **39**-8; **41**-13; **60**-30

window seat / 'wɪndo sit; 'windəʊ si:t / 靠窗座位 **60**-31

window washer / 'wɪndo waʃər; 'windəʊ wɔʃə / 抹窗工人 **21**-5

windshield / 'wɪndʃild; 'windʃi:ld / 擋風玻璃 **55**-6

windshield wiper / 'wɪndʃild waɪpər; 'windʃi:ld waipə / 雨刷 / 水撥 **55**-12

windsurfer / 'wɪndˌsɜfər; 'windˌsɜ:fə / 駕風帆者 **63**-17

windsurfing / 'wɪndˌsɜfɪŋ; 'windˌsɜ:fɪŋ / 滑浪風帆 **63**-G

windy / 'wɪndɪ; 'windi / 大風 **4**-13

wine glass / 'waɪn glæs; 'wain gla:s / 酒杯 **42**-2

wing / wɪŋ; wiŋ / 機翼 / 翼 **60**-42; **75**-27

winter / 'wɪnər; 'wintə / 冬季 **4**-3

winter sports / 'wɪntər sportz; 'wintə spɔ:tz / 冬季運動 **64**

Wisconsin / wɪs'kɑnsɪn; wis'kɔnsin / 威斯康辛 **9**

withdrawal slip / wɪð'drɔəl slip; wiðdrɔ:əl slip / 提款單 **6**-12

women s wear / 'wɪmɪnz wɛr; 'wiminz weə / 女裝 **36; 37**

woodwinds / 'wʊdwɪndz; 'wʊdˌwindz / 木管樂器 **70**-C

woodworking / 'wʊdwɜkɪŋ; 'wʊdwɜ:kiŋ / 木工 **79**-25

workbench / 'wɜkbɛntʃ; 'wɜ:kbentʃ / 工作台 **50**-22

world / wɜld; wɜ:ld / 世界 **7**

worried / 'wɜrɪd; 'wʌrid / 擔心 **32**-17

wrapping paper / 'ræpɪŋ pepər; 'ræpiŋ peɪpə / 包裝紙 **80**-26

wrench / rɛntʃ; retʃ / 扳手 **50**-9

wrestler / rɛslər; 'resələ / 摔跤者 **66**-63

wrestling / rɛslɪŋ; resəliŋ / 摔跤 **66**-G

wrist / rɪst; rist / 腕 **23**-13

write / raɪt; rait / 寫 **28**-1

Wyoming / waɪ'omɪŋ; wai'əʊmiŋ / 懷俄明 **9**

X

Xerox machine / zɪrɑks mə'ʃin; zɪərɔks mə'ʃi:n / 影印機 **20**-31

X-ray / ɛks re; eks rei / X 光 **29**-5

X-ray machine / ɛks re mə'ʃin; eks rei mə'ʃi:n / X 光機 **30**-5

xylophone / 'zaɪləˌfon; 'zailəfəʊn / 木琴 **70**-19

y

yarn / jɑrn; ja:n / 紗 / 線 **80**-4

year / jɪr; jɪə / 年 **3**-A

yellow / 'jɛlo; 'jeləʊ / 黃 **36**-23

yellow peppers / jɛlo pɛpərs; jeləʊ pepəs / 黃燈籠椒 **16**-8

yemen (Aden) / jɛmən ('edn); jemən ('eidn) / 葉門 (亞丁) **8**

yemen (Sana) / jɛmən ('sæn,ɑ); 'jemən (sɑ:'nɑ:) / 葉門 (撒納) **8**

yield / jild; ji:ld / 讓路標誌 **58**-28

yogurt / 'jogət; 'jɔgət / 酸乳酪 **13**-12

young / jʌŋ; jʌŋ / 少 **33**-15

Yugoslavia / 'jugo'slavɪə; ju:gəʊ'slɑ:vɪə / 南斯拉夫 **8**

Yukon Territory / 'jukan tɛrətorɪ; 'ju:kɔn teritri / 育康地區 **10**

Z

Zaire / za'ɪər; za:'iə / 薩伊 **8**

Zambia / 'zæmbɪə; 'zæmbiə / 尚比亞 **8**

zebra / 'zibrə; 'zibrə / 斑馬 **71**-17

Zimbabwe / zɪm'bɑbwɪ; zim'ba:bwi / 津巴布韋 **8**

zip code / zip kod; zip kəʊd / 郵遞區號碼 **19**-17

zipper / zɪpər; zipə / 拉鍊 **80**-7

zoo / zu; zu: / 動物園 **71**-A

The Photo Credits list the contributors to the *Longman Photo Dictionary* alphabetically. The bold number refers to the page on which the photograph or contributed item appears; the numbers in parentheses refer to the photograph.

A & M Records, Inc. **69** (21)
AAA **57** (1–4)
AAU/USA Junior Olympics **66** (40–43)
Alaska Division of Tourism **54** (15)
Alcoa **39** (1–11)
Ethan Allen **42** (excluding inset)
American Airlines **59** (12–17); **60** (22–33)
American Institute of Baking **21** (20)
American Cyanamid Company **76** (5)
Copyright by the American Dental Association. Reprinted by Permission. **22** (28)
American Egg Board **13** (14)
American Motors **55** (11–19, 23–24, 36, 38)
American Optometric Association **22** (29)
American Trucking Associations **57** (5–13)
(C) AMPS, 1984. **63** (3–4, 28–35); **64** (2–12, 16–17); **66** (48–56, 63–64, 66–71); **67** (13–16)
Aristokraft **45** (1–25)
Armour Processed Meat Company **18** (1)
(C) Art Attack, 1986. **12** (22–28)
Art Students League of New York. Photos by Mitchell Cherry. **22** (46); **79** (23–24)
Guy F. Atkinson Company of California. Photos by Ron Chamberlain. **21** (1); **53** (2–6)
Australian Information Service **71** (26–27)
Australian Tourist Commission **71** (25); **75** (2–3)
Ministry of Tourism, Bahamas **63** (19–20), **74** (21)
Baker's German Sweet Chocolate **17** (20)
Baldwin **70** (20)
Bank of America **6** (1–5); **22** (38)
Bechtel Power Corporation **53** (7)
Bethlehem Steel Corporation **53** (10–11)
The Bettmann Archive **33** (11–12)
Gerard Bollei **22** (40)
Boston Symphony Orchestra **69** (3–5)
E. J. Brach & Sons **3** (2)
Douglas Brkich **2** (g–j); **68** (49–52)
Jules Bucher **4** (7); **77** (7)
Van Bucher **4** (6); **11** (3–5, 7–18); **12** (20–21); **13** (9–12, 16–17); **14** (20, 22–24, F, 27–28); **15**; **16**; **17** (1, 22); **18** (6–10, 13, 15, 17–18); **21** (5–6, 13, 22); **22** (25); **30** (13, 17–18); **34** (33–36, 39–41); **39** (20); **44** (9–21); **45** (31); **48**; **54** (5–8); **56** (1–4, 11–14); **58** (20–23); **69** (19–20); **75** (21); **79** (6–11, 14, 17–18)
Bumble Bee Seafoods, Inc. **14** (18)
W. Atlee Burpee Co. **40** (14, 16–26)
California Avocado Commission **17** (5)
Campbell Soup Co. **14** (19); **17** (4)
Canadian Pacific Ltd. **56** (5–10)
Carolina Biological Supply Company **24** (51–61)
Caulk Dentsply **30** (6)
Cayman Islands Department of Tourism **63** (5–6)
CBS News **22** (32)
Charles River Lab, Inc. **76** (14)
Chase Manhattan Archives **22** (34, 37)
Chock Full o' Nuts **17** (23); **34** (27)
Ciba-Geigy **22** (24)
Citibank **6** (8); **11** (1); **12** (19); **22** (36); **53** (12–13)
City of Chicago Department of Aviation **59** (5–6)
Clairol **33** (23–24)
Bruce Coleman, Inc. **4** (5) photo © Wendell Metzen; **22** (43) photo by S.L. Craig, Jr.; **34** (25) photo by M.P. Kahl; **53** (1) photo © Wendell Metzen; **69** (16–18) photo © Michael S. Rewner; **72** (41–43) photo by Franklin J. Sanborn
Colgate-Palmolive Company **30** (12)

Cornell Laboratory of Ornithology **75** (12) photo by Allen Cruickshank; (22–23) photo by W.R. Spafford; (24–25) photos by Mike Hopiak; (28) photo by John S. Dunning
CPC International **13** (15); **14** (31)
(C) David J. Cross, 1986. **75** (1)
Dairy Goat Journal **73** (26–27)
Department of the Army **78** (1–9)
Ducks Unlimited, Inc. **75** (8–9)
Edmund Scientific Company **79** (12–13)
Harvey Eisner **21** (12)
Evenflo Juvenile Furniture Company **47** (12–13, 16)
FACT **13** (B)
Fashion Institute of Technology **22** (44–45) photo by John Senzer
Fieldcrest **43** (19–20)
Fine Woodworking **79** (25)
Florida Division of Tourism **62** (19–20); **63** (17–18, 25–27); **67** (17–21); **71** (3–5, 13–14, 24); **72** (32, 37)
Ford **55** (37)
Frito-Lay, Inc. **18** (11–12)
Gaines Dog Care Center **72** (38–40)
Gerber Products Company **47** (1–11, 14–15, 17–24)
Godfather's Pizza **18** (3)
The Great Eastern Mussel Farms, Inc. **74** (23)
Haagen-Dazs **17** (21)
Hallmark Cards **3** (1, 5–6, 11–13)
The Handweavers Guild of America **79** (19–20) photo by Hodges Glenn, Jr.
Hawaii Vistors Bureau **63** (14–16)
Grant Heilman **73** (29–30); **75** (19–20)
Hershey **18** (16)
Highway Users Federation **58** (18–19, 26–39)
H.U.D. **39** (25–31)
Hohner, Inc. **70** (21–22)
Houston Grand Opera **69** (6–7) photo by Jim Caldwell
Indiana University **65** (27–38)
International Numismatic Society **79** (1–5)
Ireland-Gannon Associates, Inc. **39** (12–14); **40** (8–13)
Japan National Tourist Organization **34** (42); **66** (65); **79** (21–22)
Joseph R. Jehl, Jr. **75** (10–11, 29–30)
George E. Joseph **69** (11–15)
Kansas City International Airport **59** (7–9, 18–20); **60** (38–43)
John F. Kennedy Library **31** (A, G)
Kenya Tourist Office **54** (16); **63** (1–2); **71** (11–12, 21); **72** (35); **75** (13)
Kick Enterprises **66** (44–47)
Aaron Kiley **55** (25–32)
Kimberly Clark Corporation **47** (25)
Kraft, Inc. **13** (13)
(C) James R. Levin, 1986. **44** (1–8)
Thomas J. Lipton, Inc. **34** (28)
(C) Los Angeles Dodgers, Inc. 1985. **65** (19–26)
Macy's **3** (12); **41**
Marriott Corporation **18** (2, 5)
Maybelline **24** (37–38)
Metropolitan Transportation Authority **57** (15, 17)
Miami Seaquarium **74** (9, 15–17)
Milton Bradley Company **79** (29)
Milwaukee Symphony Orchestra **69** (1–2)
Ji H. Min **44** (22–27)
Monkmeyer Press **21** (11) photo by Paul Conklin; **22** (39) photo by David Conklin, (42) photo by Hugh Rogers; **34** (47–48) photo by Jason Horowitz ©1985; **53** (20) photo by Hugh Rogers
Benjamin Moore **21** (4)
Murray Chris-Craft Cruisers, Inc. **63** (21–24)
Nabisco Brands, Inc. **14** (29–30)
NASA **77** (1–3, 5–6, 8–17)
National Aquarium **74** (10, 12–14, 22, 27)
National Association of Women in Construction **53** (19)
National Bowling Council **68** (34–38)
National Broiler Council **17** (14–16)

Contributors

We would like to thank the following establishments for their cooperation:

Bloomingdale's, White Plains, New York **42** (10–14)
Charles Librett Hardware, New Rochelle, New York **50**; **53** (21–23)
Daminc Jewelers, New York, New York **2**(f)
The Family Medical Group of Manhattan, New York, New York **29** (1–8)
Farrington Square Apothecary, White Plains, New York **33** (19–20)
Kinney Shoes, White Plains, New York **37** (13–21)
Mamaroneck Post Office, Mamaroneck, New York **19** (1–9)
Nathan's, Yonkers, New York **18** (19–27)
Newmark and Lewis, Scarsdale, New York **51** (6–12)
Riverdale Country School, Riverdale, New York **22** (35); **28**
Sears Roebuck and Co., White Plains, New York **43** (14–18)
YMCA, White Plains, New York **27**

Special thanks to April Cicero and David Godsey for their creativity and talent (cover and page **32**), and to all the models who volunteered their time, energy and patience.